Also by this author

50 Ways to Be a Mainer

The Best Laid Plans

28 fun stories of plans that go awry

Printed in the United States of America

Copyright © 2021 by Captain Billy C.
Print Edition

www.facebook.com/CaptainBillyC
captainbillyc@gmail.com

All rights reserved. Except as permitted under the United States Copyright Act of 1976, no part of this publication may be reproduced or distributed in any form or by any means, including photocopying, recording, or other electronic or mechanical methods, or stored in a database or retrieval system, without prior written permission of the author.

Cover Design
Nate Voellm
www.natevoellmdesign.com

Attention: The following stories are true, but the names have been changed to protect the innocent, and sometimes the guilty.

Permissions: Requests for permission to use any content in any manner from this book must be obtained in writing prior to such use. Permission may be requested by contacting Captain Billy C on his Facebook page (www.facebook.com/CaptainBillyC) or by e-mailing him at captainbillyc@gmail.com.

Dedicated to Jenni

It would be impossible to over-estimate the literary, technical, and moral support given to me by this talented woman. Without her patient assistance, this book would not be possible.

Table of Contents

About *The Best Laid Plans*...	xi
Acknowledgments	xiii
1. Lookin' for Adventure	1
2. Douglas Adams High School: Part I – Handy Frank	10
3. Douglas Adams High School: Part II – Unforgettable	18
4. Sometimes You Feel Like a Nut	27
5. Thrill and Danger: Part I – Some Kind of Hero	36
6. Thrill and Danger: Part II – Bring 'Em Back Alive	44
7. Almost Perfect	51
8. Paranoia Strikes Deep	60
9. Rapid Descent: Part I – Damn Girl Scouts!	67
10. Rapid Descent: Part II – What Could Possibly Go Wrong?	77
11. The Little Ninja that Could	87

12. A Cat in a Tree	94
13. Romance on the Beach: Part I – A Three-Hour Tour	104
14. Romance on the Beach: Part II – From the Sublime to the Ridiculous	118
15. Chatterbox	132
16. Burning Desire	140
17. Command Performance: Part I – The Poor Player	154
18. Command Performance – Part II – Interview with a Comedian	163
19. Command Performance – Part III – Itching to Be a Man	176
20. Legend in His Own Mind	182
21. Saving a Life: Part I – Damsel in Distress	189
22. Saving a Life: Part II – Shit Happens	199
23. Picture This: Part I – I See Dead People (and they're naked)	208
24. Picture This: Part II – The Great Wall of Fred	215
25. Much Ado About Nothing	223
26. Justice is Blind	231

27. Send in the Clowns – Don't Bother, They're Here	246
28. Wired for Success	257
About the Author	271
Excerpt from *50 Ways to Be a Mainer*	275

About The Best Laid Plans

NO, THE TITLE is not a quote from Shakespeare, but rather from the Scottish poet, Robert Burns. If you don't believe me, you can Google it. Nevertheless, it is appropriate to this book.

They say the gods laugh when we make plans. And all 28 short stories in this book involve the gods somehow laughing at us. We set our hopes, dreams, and desires along a certain path only to find them careening over the edge of an unseen cliff like Wile E. Coyote in his attempts to capture the Road Runner.

Our lives are filled with Wile E. Coyote-like moments that can best be summarized by his resigned despair as he stares directly at the viewer just before gravity kicks in and sends him hurtling down to the canyon below followed by a distant "thump" and a circular cloud of expanding dust. The gods then take the role of the Road Runner who peers over the edge of the cliff, smiles, and takes off with a loud "Meep Meep!" While I don't mean to suggest that falling off a cliff, literally or figuratively, is funny, watching people colossally fail in their endeavors, even with the help of overly elaborate plans and the Acme Corporation, can be humorous indeed.

Most of these stories belong to a rich oral history that is shared by the protagonist in a bar or at dinner. Details may have become blurry and situations "slightly" exaggerated. But, as any storyteller knows, these are not news reports but rather a fun way to spend some time.

Telling funny stories in bars has generally been associated with males. However, if you listen carefully you can find women regaling their companions with absolutely hysterical life experiences. In an effort to provide gender equality, approximately half the stories are based on women's lives and told from their point of view.

The stories do not appear in any particular order, although some have multiple parts. Some of them took place over fifty years ago. Some are far more recent. It's OK to start in the middle and work your way forward or backward. Or to keep this book in the bathroom to read in the porcelain library. I won't mind. But don't forget to wash your hands!

ENJOY!

Acknowledgments

EVEN EXPERIENCED WRITERS benefit from lots of support, patience, and literary criticism to complete their work. This was provided by a group of talented and generous writers without whose encouragement, suggestions, and critiques it would not have been possible for me to write this book. It is with the most heartfelt gratitude that I thank each and every one:

Bill Andrews
Ellen Brosnahan
Harold Ellis
Bob Fellman
Elliot Goodman
Ellen Marks
Joanne Schmidt
Thomas Royal Smith
Meg Spinella
Seabury Stanton
Jeff Widmer

<u>In Memorium</u>
Helga Harris

1. Lookin' for Adventure

THE BIG RED Yamaha barreled down a two-lane road in the late afternoon sun of the Arkansas Ozarks. Brad had left his home in Chicago the day before and now headed from St. Louis to Little Rock. It was hot, it was humid, and he was sweating profusely. The heat from the black engine cooked his shins. Even so, he absolutely loved his red and gold bike. It was smooth. The perfect bike, he felt, to get away from a marriage that was circling the drain. In his mind, he was singing Steppenwolf's *Born to be Wild*. He was definitely "looking for adventure" or whatever came his way.

What came his way was a tall redhead with tight black jeans and a low-cut black and silver silk blouse. She stood on the side of the road with her thumb out. After a micro-second of internal debate, he hit the brakes, did a U-turn, then another, and came back to her. He was surprised. At 61 miles per hour, she looked good indeed. But from a dead stop, not so much. While she was thin, with ample cleavage, the valley view was spoiled by a large zit asymmetrically located on the right slope. She was older than he expected, and her lined face looked like she had smoked too many cigarettes in the strong Arkansas sun. She reminded him of an old baseball glove that had been left out in the rain one too many times. Her teased, almost abused, hair was a semi-attractive shade of artificial red that has never occurred in nature.

"Where're you goin'?" he asked.

Without waiting for an invitation, she immediately climbed on the bike, and replied, "Any ol' place you are, honey! I jus' left my husband and I gotta get away!"

Uh oh, he thought. *Too damn late to look for adventure somewhere else.*

She wrapped her arms around him and gave him a tighter squeeze than necessary. "What's your name, baby?"

"Brad"

"Well, Brad, my name is Anna Mae. And we better git goin', darlin'. My husband's shore to be pissed."

Brad twisted the throttle and took off like a

ten-point buck in hunting season. The South scared him. He had only been south of the Mason Dixon line once in his life when he was twelve years old. Seeing the signs for "colored" and "white" washrooms and drinking fountains during that trip left an indelible fear and anger in his young mind. Although he was white, he grew up in a mixed-race neighborhood and he couldn't understand how people could be so unfair and cruel. As he got older, his image of the south contained stories about church bombings and civil rights demonstrations in Little Rock. He also remembered three civil rights workers from up north being murdered by the Ku Klux Klan. Yeah, the South scared him.

Brad tended to think in movie images. His mind pictured one of the last scenes from the movie *Electra-Glide in Blue* where Robert Blake got blown off his motorcycle by a shotgun blast. Or *Easy Rider* where a severe beating by locals killed Jack Nicholson's character. Apparently, bikers didn't do well in movies. Or in real life, either. He recalled an article written about a month ago in the *Chicago Sun-Times*: "Three Bikers Killed in Trinity Texas." Nobody would say why, but apparently, the bikers had annoyed the locals.

And here he was, with a married woman who had just left her husband, perched on the back of his motorcycle. What could possibly go wrong?

"Shit," he mumbled to himself. "Shit, shit, shit, shit, shit! What to do, what to do?"

The bike negotiated the curves, hills, and valleys with little trouble. He wanted to go faster but cruised at just sixty-one miles per hour. He felt that was probably as fast as he dared go without having an awkward conversation with a sunglass-wearing, pot-bellied, gum-popping, local sheriff, like in *In the Heat of the Night*. After all, Jimmy Carter had just imposed a national speed limit of fifty-five to help stave off the gas crisis.

As he rounded a curve, he saw a totally nondescript, windowless, cement-block building with a big neon sign that, redundantly enough, said "ROADHOUSE BAR." Brad figured he might be able to get Anna Mae drunk and leave her at the bar, so he hit the brakes on the bike and pulled into the gravel parking lot full of well-used pickup trucks. He hated gravel. Turning fast on gravel was a sure way to dump your bike. So, he circled the lot slowly, pulled into the second row between two rusted and dented trucks, and pointed the bike back toward the road. If he had to leave in a hurry, he didn't want to have to negotiate a fast turn on the loose gravel.

He looked back over his shoulder and asked, "Anna Mae, want a drink?"

"That sounds good, baby!"

He took off his helmet and led Anna Mae into the bar. It was big! And it was so cold he could feel the perspiration immediately start to evaporate off his body. It was dimly lit so it took his eyes a while to adjust. As he struggled to see through the cloud of cigarette smoke, his eyes began to sting. He could feel his lungs contract.

When his vision finally adjusted, he noticed that there were several pool tables, all being used, and a group of locals sitting around a large round table. The bar was decorated with a flair for the macabre. Numerous dead animals hung on the walls. In the corner stood a stuffed black bear with a cub at her feet. Dozens of deer, fish, and a jack-a-lope stared back at him. The biggest Confederate flag he had ever seen was draped on the wall behind the bar. In the corner by the pool tables, an art deco Rock-Ola jukebox full of chrome and changing colored lights was playing "El Paso" by Marty Robbins. *Great*, he thought, *A guy gets shot by an angry mob of cowboys over a woman*. He was definitely nervous.

He planned to make a quiet entrance, but then Anna Mae exclaimed loudly, "Hey boys, this here's my new boyfriend, Brad! I left that bastard Jackson, and Brad here came to my rescue." Was it his imagination, or had the bar suddenly gone deathly quiet? Nope, it wasn't his imagination. Her arm snaked around his waist and her hand slowly drifted lower to his ass.

Shit, shit, shit, shit, shit! So much for going unnoticed.

He wanted to sit by the door in case he had to make a fast exit, but there was no room, so he had to sit at the far end of the bar with Anna Mae. He looked around and saw that everyone was drinking Budweiser. He hated Budweiser but ordered one anyway.

Best to blend in.

He sat there nursing his beer and watched Anna Mae light cigarette after cigarette. As he listened to her prattle on about something or other, he realized this was not her first drink of the day. He was quietly trying to figure out how he was going to leave her at the bar without making a scene and dangerously annoying the locals and winding up being the star of his own country and western song.

As he finished his first beer, Brad was just starting to relax at the bar when he heard from the round table, "Hey, boy."

Oh shit. Maybe if I ignore it, it will go away.

"Hey you, Brad! Get over here, boy!"

He left a couple of dollars on the bar and sauntered over to the round table with the five locals. He desperately tried to look nonchalant.

A tall, rangy-looking fellow asked, "That your bike out there?"

"Yep."

"You ain't from around here."

"Nope."

"Well, where are you FROM, boy?" he asked with a mixture of annoyance and exasperation.

"I'm from Chicago." *You know, Land of Lincoln, that should really help!*

"So, where you headed?"

"Little Rock today. Houston tomorrow to see my brother." He thought by mentioning another southern state, he might fit in better.

"What, are you crazy, boy? Ride all that way on a bike?"

"I've been called worse."

"Me too. Well sit down, let me buy you a

beer."

Brad sat. Several voices assaulted him at once.

"Do you need a place to stay?"

"There's a room in the back of the bar if you need it."

"That's a purty bike. What kind is it?"

"Why'd you buy that rice-burner instead of a Harley?"

"Here, let me get you another beer."

In thirty seconds, Brad went from a self-perceived crime victim to a minor celebrity and guest. After an hour of drinks and conversation about the merits of "rice burners" vs. "rock-crushing Harleys," Ford vs. Chevy pick-up trucks, the discussion finally landed on Anna Mae. Brad glanced over to where she was still sitting. She was now surrounded by several other men and seemed to be getting along like long-lost cousins – kissing cousins at that. Eddie, the tall rangy one, noticed his glance and said "Aw hell, don't worry none about Anna Mae. She does this all the time. One of us'll git her home."

Brad tried not to grimace as he sucked down the last of his third or fourth Budweiser. He slowly stood and said his goodbyes. He had a schedule to keep and besides, he didn't want to meet Anna Mae's "pissed off" husband. He left the coolness of the bar, staggered to his bike, and "headed down the highway."

His helmet hid the broad grin on his face and muffled his voice as he sang to himself, "Lookin' for adventure…"

2. Douglas Adams High School: Part I
Handy Frank

DENISE DELEO PLOPPED down in the chair across from new teacher Bonnie O'Reilly in the faculty cafeteria. She set her Douglas Adams High School plastic tray directly in front of her. She could see the cartoonish dolphin's face, emblazoned on the tray, peeking out at her from under her food. It had been a long walk from her classroom because it was the cafeteria at the end of the school.

Denise viewed Bonnie as a younger sister and chose to take her under her wing. Although the school provided Bonnie with an official mentor, Denise provided more useful information, like who could be trusted, who should be avoided, and, most importantly, who was single. Because they shared a common lunch period, they chose to sit together almost every day, and now, only two weeks into the school year, they had grown close.

"You gotta love Taco Tuesday!" Denise exclaimed.

"How're you doing?" Bonnie asked. "How are your classes going?"

"They're all OK, except for third period which is full of a bunch of perverts. Sophomore humor is, well, sophomoric at best."

Bonnie bit into her taco and washed it down with cafeteria milk.

Denise looked at her and asked, "Why didn't you get a Diet Coke or something like that?

"I'm trying to eat healthy."

"Hey, I'm a health teacher. Trust me. Warm cafeteria milk ain't all that healthy! You're better off with the chemicals in a Diet Coke."

"Actually, I'd prefer a fine Negro Modelo with tacos."

Denise responded, in a mock haughty tone, "For me, I would choose the bouquet of a Dos Equis."

They sat quietly, crunching on their tacos. Then Bonnie said, "Denise, I was wondering…"

"Bonnie, you've gotta stop calling me Denise. Call me DD like everyone else does. It's based on my initials, so you should be able to remember it."

"Well, I'll try, DD. But don't call me by my

initials. Bonnie O'Reilly translates to BO and I don't need that moniker!"

"I can see where that would be a problem," Denise snickered. "Sorry I interrupted. What were you wondering?"

"Well, I was wondering about the naked man right outside the cafeteria."

"Naked man? Oh, boy! Where?" Denise exclaimed as she pretended to get up to go searching for the man.

"DD, I'm talking about the statue that's in the courtyard by the student cafeteria. You know, it's behind the wall of windows, but tucked away in the corner so you barely notice it."

"Oh, you mean *Arriving Man*."

"That's its name?"

"Yep. It's a long story, but you're a history teacher, so I figure you're used to long stories. He's named *Arriving Man* because if you look at him, he looks like he's coming out of a wall or the dark or something. He's in midstride with one arm down and the other arm in front of him raised high as if he's reaching for something. Reaching for the stars, I guess. It's supposed to be inspirational. Anyway..." she stopped for a moment to drink some of her Diet Coke, then continued. "The school was built in the early '70s. And there was a lot of publicity about how modern and efficient it would be. It was the first air-conditioned building in the school district. Some rich guy artist, sculptor actually, donated *Arriving Man* to the new school. It's made out of bronze and it's worth more than your first three month's salary. When he donated it, he said he hoped to provide inspiration for the students. And it did, just not the way he thought. He certainly fostered their creativity."

"He's naked. So why did the school board take it?"

"In many ways, the artist was passive-aggressive. He put the district in a double bind. If they took the statue, they would be presenting their students with an anatomically correct, naked man emerging from a wall. While this is a fairly liberal community, or at least it was back then, they were afraid of possible conservative or religious backlash. You know, the 'sex is dirty, save it for someone you love' crowd. On the other hand, if they politely refused to take the statue, because of his nudity, they were afraid there would be a backlash by the liberals who would compare the board members to book-burning

Nazis afraid of pictures of Michelangelo's *David*. So, as Simon and Garfunkle sang, 'every way you look at it you lose.' Weirdly enough, *Arriving Man* is actually a better-proportioned statue than *David*. Slightly better hung, too."

"You're terrible, DD. Funny, but terrible."

"Hey, I resemble that!" Denise clutched at her chest in mock offense. "Anyway, as I was saying, the school board couldn't decide what to do. Finally, a compromise was reached. They would take the statue gratefully, smuggle it into the building, and hide it in the corner of the enclosed courtyard next to the student cafeteria. The hope was, even though the students could see it, because of its out-of-the-way location, they would ignore it. And, more importantly, both the conservatives and the liberals wouldn't be reminded of it because it wasn't planted in front of the building. But, two thousand high school students, with all of their hormones raging, coupled with their social awkwardness and creativity would never let the statue be. Every year something happens. And although it's vandalism, I have to admire their ingenuity."

"Vandalism? What did they do?"

"Being new to the building, you missed some

great ones that I'm sure you'll hear about several times before the year is up. But allow me to be the first," she continued. "Several years ago, some art students were able to get past the locked door and into the courtyard with a tub of red clay. *Arriving Man* suddenly became better hung than Long Dong Silver, the porn star from the '70s. And let me say, he looked very happy to see you! They put a sign around his neck indicating he was no longer *Arriving Man*, he was *Cuming Man*. Another year they painted his balls blue. Then one year, his dick was silver. Another year, it was gold. And, did you notice how his arm is outstretched? I can't tell you the number of times they put lit cigarettes in his hand. One year, they even put a lit joint between his fingers. But that's not the best of it.

"In my opinion, the best story involves the dean/football coach, Frank Butkowski. Frank was a giant of a man. He played varsity football as a Cornhusker at Nebraska. He retired a few years ago, so you'll probably never meet him. But he was big! And he was bald. He just had a few patches of gray fuzz by his temples. But the top of his head was as smooth and large as a bowling ball. It was just as shiny, too. He always wore polo shirts that showed off his chest and biceps.

"One day, at the end of fourth period, several students were staring out the window at *Arriving Man* and laughing. Frank was immediately angry. He knew something was up and he raced to the locked door that was supposed to keep every student out of the area. He found the door open, rushed out to *Arriving Man*, and saw him wearing a condom."

"At least there was safe sex," Bonnie grinned and interjected.

DD chuckled. "Frank walked over to *Arriving Man* and attempted to pull the condom off. Unfortunately for Frank, the students put it on with Super Glue. And all he was able to do was to stretch the condom out. Feeling frustrated, he began pulling at the condom, hoping to dislodge it." She paused. "Have you ever gotten that feeling that you're being watched? Frank stopped rubbing and tugging and looked over his shoulder. He saw that the fifth-period lunch group had arrived, all four hundred of them, and they were now plastered against the bank of windows overlooking the courtyard, staring at him as he gave *Arriving Man* a 'hand job.' His bald head and sweaty face turned bright red and he tried to get really small and slink away unnoticed, not at all oblivious to the laughter and shouts of encouragement by the hundreds of students who were mobbed up against the windows, in some places more than ten deep, all struggling to get a better view. As he exited the courtyard, his enraptured audience burst into a round of enthusiastic applause and shouted 'More, more' as if they were at a concert hoping for an encore. It's alleged that Frank ran back to his office, turned off the lights, locked the door, and just sat there. Some people say that he was so distraught that he hid under his desk. But I never believed that... He was way too big. From then on, the students nicknamed him 'Handy Frank'."

Both women laughed. Just then the bell rang, so they picked up their trays and put them on the receiving counter to be cleaned and processed.

Bonnie said, "You know, DD, I'll never get that picture out of my head." They laughed some more and headed off to class.

3. Douglas Adams High School: Part II
Unforgettable

"JOHN, ANYTHING SPECIAL on the schedule this week?"

"Nothing particularly difficult, Senator. Mostly meeting with contributors, lobbyists, and so on. Friday, though, you're scheduled to make a speech at Douglas Adams High School."

"I'm not real familiar with that school. Can you get me some background on it? Something that makes the school special. By the way, where is it?"

"About twenty miles northwest of O'Hare, Senator."

"Why am I doing this speech again, John?"

"It's in a growing suburb, Senator. And politically, it seems to be evenly divided between Republicans and Democrats. So, by talking to the students you might pick up a few votes from the parents and from the students themselves when they're old enough. Also, if you're thinking of running for president in '88, you really need to be out in public every chance you get. Local press coverage is better than no press coverage, sir."

"I guess that makes sense. I'll probably just do a variation on speech number two, but I need you to punch it up a bit. Get me some information about the school please."

John scurried out of the senator's office and headed for his own much smaller office. He went over his schedule for the day and decided he had enough time to call the school directly. He didn't need to talk to the principal. Many times, the school secretary would provide more useful information than the boss. Administrators tended to become long-winded and try to impress you with how absolutely great they'd been at making the school a standout.

Two Days Later

JOHN KNOCKED ON the senator's office door and the senator beckoned him in. "Come in, John. Come on in." The senator seemed to be in a good mood today.

The senator's office on Michigan Ave. in downtown Chicago was large with a picture window overlooking Grant Park. To the right, he could see Buckingham Fountain and, in the distance, Adler Planetarium. Beyond the park, beautiful Lake Michigan stretched almost all the way to the horizon. On a clear day, the senator could see Indiana. His office was sparsely furnished. In the center was a large mahogany desk and to the side were numerous matching bookshelves. One was filled with blue and silver volumes of *Corpus Juris Secundum*, a perfect prop for a lawmaker's office. On the other side hung portraits of Abraham Lincoln, John F. Kennedy, Martin Luther King, Jr., and Bobby Kennedy.

"Good morning, Senator. I have the information for the speech on Friday at the high school."

"Ah, yes, John. What have you got?"

"It's a typical northwest suburban high school, sir. Approximately 1850 students. Almost entirely white. Above-average ACT and SAT scores. And a high percentage of students do attend college."

"Good, John, good. But what makes them special?"

"Well, at first I couldn't find anything particular about the school, other than they have an unusual piece of art, called *Arriving Man*, in one of their courtyards that I'd advise you not to mention. But then I found out that they have a very large population of hearing impaired and deaf students."

"Really? Why?"

"They belong to a consortium of about ten high schools and they divide up the severe and profoundly disabled students into certain categories so they can give them specialized services easier. Douglas Adams is the center for the hearing-impaired program. One of the other schools in the area services the physically handicapped and another the blind. So, Adams High School has about fifty hearing impaired and deaf students and a fair number of interpreters and sign language teachers. They've actually become quite well known in the Chicago area for their program, and parents move to the area if they have a deaf child, just to be part of the school. When you deliver your speech, there will be an interpreter standing off to your left, signing to those students. By the way, they'll be sitting right up front so it's easier for them to read your lips and see the interpreter's hands."

"Good work, John. How do you suggest I acknowledge this without seeming to pander to them?"

"I think the best approach, sir, would be if you would sign a simple greeting to them. It wouldn't have to be long or elaborate. Just a simple greeting."

"That's great, John, except I don't know how to sign."

"I've thought of that too, Senator. I have a cousin who knows how to sign and lives close to our office. She'd be happy to teach you something simple. I can have her here by the end of the day if you'd like."

"Let me see...how about 5 o'clock?"

"I'm sure that will work, sir."

John walked back to his office and called his cousin to solidify her tutorial appointment with the senator.

Friday Afternoon

THE PRINCIPAL STOOD behind a podium that was emblazoned with the dolphin logo of the school's mascot as he waited for everyone to enter and be seated. He was wearing his best brown suit with a crisply pressed white shirt and an orange tie. Brown, white, and orange were the school's colors. There was a bit of controversy about the choice of brown and orange as the school colors. But, the administrator who undemocratically picked them was a big fan of Cleveland football – much to the dismay of the cheerleaders who never felt that they looked good in brown and orange and who had trouble finding outfits with those colors to wear on school spirit days. They also disliked the colors because it was difficult to come up with a cheer that rhymed with orange. Actually, it wasn't difficult. It was impossible.

The entire student body and faculty were gathered in the gymnasium, the only room in the school large enough to house the multitude. All the bleachers were pulled out on the sides of the gym and hundreds of aluminum folding chairs were placed in geometrically straight lines over the entire basketball court. Teachers and administrators were strategically scattered amongst the students to help maintain order. The hearing-impaired students were seated behind the first row, which was reserved for school board members, the superintendent, and several district-level administrators. There were a few members of the press accompanied by staff photographers in the back. Once the speeches began, the photographers would rush toward the stage and snap close-ups of the event for the local papers. There were no television cameras present. After all, this was an address to a high school, not a major policy speech.

The gymnasium glowed orange under the sodium-vapor lights and, unfortunately, smelled exactly like a gymnasium. Every day, sweaty, hormonal teenagers ran up and down the court playing basketball, volleyball, badminton, etc. adding a particular fragrance that the noisy ventilator fans could never completely eliminate. To make matters worse, whenever there was a large event, the ventilator fans had to be shut off because their constant roar would drown out the speakers. The heat, the humidity, and the smell from over 2,000 warm bodies began to build.

The principal raised his hands to silence the crowd. The crowd's roar slowly subsided, partially out of respect for the man, but also because of the threatening stares of the teachers. He began an overly long introduction of their speaker, emphasizing how lucky everyone in the audience was to see the esteemed senator from Illinois.

The senator strode confidently up to the podium. He smiled at the crowd and waited for the applause to die down. He was not an imposing figure. Not very tall, rather thin, wearing a dark grey suit, white shirt, and his signature black bowtie. His horn-rimmed glasses reminded the older people in the audience of the actor Wally Cox, who played Mr. Peepers.

He began to speak. As he did so, he looked directly at the deaf-ed students in the first few rows and signed to them as he said, "I'm so happy to meet you." This is where a problem arose. Perhaps John's cousin wasn't quite as good at teaching sign language as she thought. Or, perhaps the senator forgot exactly what he was taught. Or maybe even it was just a slight flick of the wrists. Regardless, the senator did not quite sign "meet you." By turning his wrists a mere ninety degrees, he signed, "I'm so happy to fuck you."

The interpreter standing to his left and slightly behind began signing vigorously, even though the senator wasn't talking. "DON'T YOU LAUGH. DON'T YOU DARE LAUGH. HE'S REALLY TRYING. DON'T YOU LAUGH."

The deaf students and the faculty who knew how to sign did their best not to laugh as the senator launched into "speech #2." It contained all the elements one would expect. "Proud of their hard work... Bright future... Becoming an adult... Reach for the stars... The future lies ahead... Blah, blah blah..." It was a nice speech – full of platitudes and eminently forgettable. And it ended with polite and semi-enthusiastic applause.

John ushered the senator quickly out a side door where the senator's black Lincoln Town Car was waiting. As they settled into the back seat, John, as always, complimented the senator. "Great job, sir. I'm sure the students will all remember it."

The senator agreed. "I'm sure they will. Did you notice the smiles on the deaf students' faces when I signed to them? It was really refreshing. They smiled at me through the entire speech. I'm sure they won't forget me."

"I'm sure they won't, senator. I'm sure they won't. You were unforgettable."

4. Sometimes You Feel Like a Nut

CAL STOOD FACING the mirror. He couldn't decide if he was finished dressing or not. He wore a dark blue shirt, black pants, and a caramel-colored sport jacket. Should he wear a tie? He decided against it. He looked in the mirror at his face. He had a dark complexion with Mediterranean coloring and a mildly hooked nose and a full, black beard. On any given day he could pass for Italian, Greek, Israeli, or even Egyptian. The fact that he was German surprised everyone. He was as far away from the blonde, blue-eyed look as can possibly be imagined.

He glanced at his watch and saw that he had fifteen minutes, so he bounded down the stairs and headed out the front door. He didn't want to be late picking up Katherine. After all, it was the all-important third date.

He barely noticed his car as he hopped in, which was somewhat surprising because everyone else did. It was a "baby-crap" yellow and rusted Datsun B-210. Cal viewed his car as an appliance. Its sole function was to get from point A to B. He did not derive any status from the vehicle he drove. While most of the rust was consigned to rocker panels and lower fenders, an odd thing about the Datsun was that it had a huge rust spot on the roof. Fixing it would have been prohibitively expensive, and economically stupid. The Datsun B-210 certainly wasn't worth much and rust repair would have cost far more than the vehicle was worth. But somehow, he came to possess a large, metallic, red, white, and blue STP Oil Treatment sticker. Being artistically inclined, he plastered it over the large rust spot on the roof. Problem solved. Andy Granatelli would be so proud. All in all, the car drove remarkably well, especially considering its appearance. Sadly, the B-210 was only a few years old. Like most of its Datsun brothers, the sheet metal on the car was so thin that several of them had developed rust on their trip to the U.S. from Japan.

After a short, uneventful drive, Cal arrived at Katherine's small bungalow. He walked up the steps to her front door, rang the doorbell, and twenty seconds later, Katherine appeared at the door. She looked beautiful. Katherine was of Scandinavian descent and looked every bit of it. She was tall, blue-eyed, and had a very full head of wavy strawberry-blonde hair. Her complexion was so white, she was almost translucent. Her whole body, at least what he could see of it, was covered with freckles. She had an infectious smile. She greeted Cal with a warm hug. She told him, "You look really nice."

When Cal pulled away from her embrace, he noticed her bright green, form-fitting dress. The jewel tone of her outfit set her hair ablaze with highlights. "Wow," was all he could manage. She closed the door behind her, and they walked hand in hand to the right side of the car. Cal, being somewhat old-fashioned, opened the door for her, partly because he was a gentleman but mostly so he could stare at her legs as she struggled with her short dress to modestly get in the car. He climbed in the driver's side and they headed off to the Wellington Steak House, leaving a trail of pale, blue smoke.

They pulled up in front of the restaurant. Cal got out of his car and started to race around to open Katherine's door, hoping for another peek at her legs, but she was too fast for him and opened the door and hopped out on her own. The restaurant valet took Cal's keys, looked at the Datsun with dismay, and then looked at Cal as if to say, "Really…?" But Cal was oblivious to the valet's silent rebuke. Even if he had noticed, he wouldn't have cared. "Function over form" was his motto.

They walked arm in arm into the restaurant. They confirmed their reservation, and the maître d' escorted them to a booth near the far wall of the dining room. After receiving their menus from the maître d', Katherine stated matter-of-factly, "I don't know about you, but I'm really hungry."

Cal responded, "Me too. I could eat a whole cow!"

Katherine looked around the room. She could see white tablecloths, burgundy leather booths and chairs, candles at every table, and heavy cutlery carefully placed at each setting. Stained glass windows were surrounded by red brocade drapes. "This place is beautiful!" she exclaimed.

They looked over the lengthy wine list and decided to order a bottle of Beaujolais. While they shared a common desire to have a good meal and to get to know each other better, their secondary agendas were slightly different. Katherine really wanted to get to know Cal. She had already decided she liked what she saw and was starting to feel more and more comfortable with him. She was uncertain as to whether she could trust him enough to allow further intimacy. She wore a matching bra and panties, just in case. Cal, on the other hand, had trouble concentrating on the conversation as he was more interested in how the date would end. Would there be a chaste kiss goodbye at the doorway? An open-mouthed game of dueling tongues? Or perhaps an invitation for a "cup of coffee" in her living room? After all, it was their third date and, well, some "coffee" was a reasonable expectation.

They both ordered Beef Wellington, the house specialty, with side salads. They would decide on dessert later. The time between ordering and their dinners arriving was filled with conversation. Katherine recounted how she had been an elementary school teacher for ten years. She loved her job because she really loved the children. As she said this, she watched for his reaction. Cal responded that he loved children too, but he was much more comfortable with older kids which is why he worked as a high school counselor. He then switched topics, trying to impress her with tales of his athletic prowess as a baseball pitcher in college and local tennis star. The conversation continued smoothly while the salad was served along with warm bread and honey butter.

As they ate, the banter continued, then stopped abruptly. Cal had an obviously pained look on his face. Katherine looked at him quizzically and asked, "Is something wrong?"

Cal said, "I'm not sure. It'll pass in a minute." But he began to shift uncomfortably in his seat. The remainder of his salad and his warm bread sat idly in front of him.

Katherine, with a look of concern on her face, continued to eat her salad. Cal tried to continue the conversation, but his voice was strained, and it was clear that his concentration was elsewhere. Katherine stopped eating. "Cal, what's wrong?"

Cal had begun sweating and said, "I'm not sure. My gut just feels terrible."

"Was there something in the salad that didn't agree with you?"

"I don't think so. It just came on all of a sudden. Food poisoning's fast, but not that fast."

Katherine asked, "Are you allergic to something?"

"Yeah, shellfish and shrimp, but there weren't any of them in the salad. And it doesn't feel like a food allergy. My gut just feels awful."

Katherine took his hand, looked him in the eye, and said, "Why don't you try going to the bathroom."

Unfortunately, she used the tone of voice that an elementary school teacher would use on one of her sick third graders. Cal pulled back abruptly and said, "Nah, it'll be alright." Just then the waiter arrived with their Beef Wellingtons. The food smelled delicious, and Cal felt nauseous.

Katherine, being aware of Cal's discomfort, suggested once again, "Why don't you try going to the bathroom."

Cal was embarrassed and mortified, but said "OK," and walked rather painfully to the bathroom. He knew he didn't have to pee, so he found an empty stall, stepped inside, closed the door, and leaned his head on it. He couldn't believe how badly his gut was cramping and how miserable and embarrassed he felt. He pushed back from the door, pulled down his pants, went to pull down his "tighty-whities" and let out a shriek. His briefs only went down so far and halted, being yanked inside out. Somehow, a small hole had formed in the crotch of his briefs and his left testicle had popped through and was being slowly strangled by the surrounding material. He couldn't believe it! While still sweating, he very carefully widened the hole and gingerly pushed the testicle back inside his underwear.

Few medical procedures can relieve so much pain, so completely, and so instantly. His breathing slowed, returning to normal, and he reached down and pulled up his briefs and pants and left the stall. As he washed his hands and face, he faced another dilemma. He was now ravenous, and the Beef Wellington was waiting for him on his plate! But if he ran out there and started wolfing down his food like he really wanted to, he was afraid Katherine would think he went into the bathroom and took the most ferocious dump known to mankind. Or, if he went back and told her the truth it would be embarrassing on several fronts. How do you explain to a new woman in your life about your testicle popping through a hole in your underwear, or justify the fact that even though your underwear was REAL OLD it still seemed to work fine so why buy a new pair, without looking like a slob or incredibly cheap?

So, he chose to calmly return to the table and say he was feeling a bit better and, with amazingly great restraint, slowly began to eat his dinner.

Katherine being the wise woman that she was, completely dropped that subject and asked him to tell her more about his tennis playing.

After dinner, and dessert, they went back to her house for a great "cup of coffee." They have continued having "coffee" now for over thirty years.

5. Thrill and Danger: Part I
Some Kind of Hero

CONTRARY TO PHYSICAL appearance, Officer Joe was not a "standard issue" policeman. Physically, he was about as standard issue as you can get. Average height, weight, brown hair, brown eyes – absolutely nothing to set him apart from his "brothers of the badge." What differentiated him was his mind and attitude. Before becoming a policeman, Joe was a draftsman and inventor. He had the ability to see things differently than most people.

Joe became a police officer because he wanted to help people. He wasn't in it for the glory, for the adventure, or the power. He got in trouble with his sergeant several times for failing to write tickets. It wasn't that he was lazy. He would stop people and give them a warning ticket (no fines or points against their license) or a stern lecture about their driving habits. He would tell his friends, "I just don't want to ruin anybody's day."

The few tickets he did issue were to people who personally annoyed him. For example, he gave a ticket to a man who was falling asleep at the wheel early in the morning and just missed hitting his squad car in a head-on crash.

He was honest, but he did confess that he took a bribe once. He stopped a car full of nuns for running a stop sign but, having grown up Catholic, he could not possibly give the nuns a ticket. They were so grateful they gave him a bunch of holy cards, so he figured when he died, he'd have that going for him.

Joe was also a medal-winning hero. According to the newspaper accounts, he single-handedly captured four armed robbers. But this adventure did not play out like an episode of *NCIS* or *S.W.A.T.*

It was a warm, July, Friday evening and Joe decided he was hungry and sleepy, so he headed to a local eatery for something to eat and a strong cup of coffee. He pulled the microphone from the dashboard and radioed in, "This is Elmhurst 24. I'm 10-17 at Burger Shack." In the mid-80s, Elmhurst police still used a 10-code system, and 10-17 meant he was taking a break.

The dispatcher responded, "Wait one, 24...,

armed robbery in progress Burger Shack! ... Four black males armed with a shotgun."

Joe's first thought was, *There can't be an armed robbery in progress. I'm here.* At that moment a light blue Cadillac with four black males made a right turn immediately in front of his squad car. Joe had to slam on the brakes to avoid hitting the Cadillac. Just behind the driver, he saw one of the men with the barrel of a shotgun sticking up. To him, it looked like a cannon. He immediately turned on his lights and began the pursuit. His second thought was, *Oh, shit*. He grabbed the microphone off the dash, stretching the accordion cord to bring it close to his mouth. Although it probably didn't help, he yelled into the microphone.

"Suspects heading eastbound, eastbound on St. Charles Rd."

Joe reached down to toggle the switch on the siren box which was located on the floor of his Ford Crown Victoria squad car. The siren made such a racket, Joe could not hear the dispatcher's reply. He wasn't even sure they had heard him.

"Right turn, right turn! Suspects heading south on Spring Rd." The siren continued to blare, and the tires squealed.

"Left turn, left turn! East on Vallette."

"Right turn, right turn, south on Mitchell."

The Cadillac's speed approached 60-miles-per-hour on the side streets. Joe was in hot pursuit, following closely behind. The Cadillac was turning every two blocks in the hope of losing the pursuing squad car.

"Right turn, right turn! West on Madison."

The Cadillac blew past a stop sign and sped across Spring Rd., which is a much busier road than the side streets they were on previously. Joe slowed his squad car to avoid hitting any innocent vehicles. At the same time, he did not want to slow so much that he would lose the fleeing Cadillac. In between each radio transmission, he would drop his microphone onto his lap and pick it up again to announce each rapid change of direction.

"Right turn, right turn! Heading north on Hillside."

"Left turn, left turn! Heading east on Montrose, no, NO, west on Montrose, west on Montrose." The siren continued to blare, and the tires continued to squeal. He began to smell the overheated brakes that he had to slam on before each turn.

"Left turn, left turn! South on Fairfield."

Somehow, in all of the high-speed left and right turns, Joe's microphone cord got tangled up in the steering wheel and gearshift lever, and in his attempts to extricate the cord he made the situation worse. The microphone was now "short-corded" and in order to be heard clearly by the dispatcher he had to move his head in circles, mimicking the steering wheel's turns. The results of his actions left a spider web of microphone cord stretched between the dashboard, the column shifter, and his steering wheel that was beginning to interfere with his driving.

"Turning left, left! Heading east on Vallette."

The Cadillac attempted to turn right onto the next street, but the street, in fact, was a driveway into a church parking lot. The driver, realizing that this was a dead-end parking lot, immediately jerked his wheel to the left. But physics being what it is, his momentum carried him sideways into a large oak tree.

Joe slammed on his brakes to avoid t-boning the left side of the Cadillac. "Crash, crash! Epiphany Lutheran Church, Epiphany Lutheran Church on Vallette! They're bailing out!" The perpetrators stumbled from the left side of the car; the right side being embedded in the tree trunk.

The siren was still screaming as Joe screeched to a halt, mere feet from the Cadillac. Because of the noise of the siren, he still didn't know if anyone had heard his call for backup. He tried to do several things at once: open the squad's left door, get out of the car and kneel behind the door, continue to broadcast his location, remove the Glock from his holster, and flick off the gun's safety. This was one task too many. The microphone cord somehow snagged his brand-new Glock semi-automatic handgun and flung it into the air directly in front of his face. His mind froze. He could see every detail of the gun as it spun, in a slow-motion cartwheel fashion, only inches from his nose. The gun then hit the floor, bounced, and slid under his seat.

Joe finished exiting the car and kneeled on the pavement behind the car's door. He wondered briefly if the door was strong enough to protect him from a shotgun blast. In the meantime, his right hand was frantically searching under the seat for his weapon. The four men had completed exiting the Cadillac and slowly began to move toward the squad car. He did not see their shotgun, but his racing mind panicked. *Oh, fuck! If I don't find my gun, I'm going to have to get back in my car and run away from these fools!*

He yelled at the men, "Halt, or I'll shoot." They continued to move forward. He realized they couldn't hear him above the siren. He reached into the middle of the car, switched it off, and, with his ears ringing from the blare of the sirens, repeated, "Halt, or I'll shoot."

He continued to search for his gun under the seat and his fingers brushed against something metallic. He reached in a little further and pulled out his Glock. He quickly took aim at the man closest to him. **"I said, halt or I'll shoot! Hands in the air! Hands in the air!"** The men froze in their tracks and raised their hands. Joe was afraid he would shit his pants but was able to literally contain himself.

At that moment, every squad in the western suburbs descended upon the scene. What they saw was Joe single-handedly capturing four armed robbers. It was only later discovered, unbeknownst to Joe, that the men had thrown the shotgun out the window in an attempt to prove their innocence by semi-creatively claiming, "Hey, it wasn't us. Gun? We don't have no stinkin' gun!"

One month later

THE CEREMONY WAS a pleasant enough affair. The chief of police and the mayor both gave longer than necessary speeches on Joe being a "fine example of heroism in the police force" and how the community "owed a debt of gratitude," blah, blah, blah. The newspaper wrote a complimentary article, also describing Joe's valor. The picture of him receiving his medal was a nice touch.

Joe was a humble man and did not consider himself a hero. He felt he did not deserve the medal because of the mishap with his gun. But even with that mishap, Joe did show bravery and stood his ground even when he was temporarily disarmed by an errant microphone cord. So, in a very real sense, he was "some kind of hero."

6. Thrill and Danger: Part II
Bring 'Em Back Alive

CONTRARY TO FORMULAIC police stories on TV, most police never fire their gun except at the firing range. This evening would be different for Officer Joe (yeah, the same Officer Joe from the previous story).

It was a warm, dusky October evening when Joe's squad car screeched to a halt. He and several other officers were responding to an armed robbery at a liquor store. The suspect, who was reported to be fleeing on foot, was described as white and big with a light-colored jacket. Joe immediately saw several officers chasing a big guy in a light-colored jacket across a large, empty parking lot. For a big guy, he was moving very fast and slowly putting more distance between him and the chasing officers. They were running across Joe's path about ten yards away.

Joe pulled out his Glock and yelled, "Halt, or I'll shoot." The cops who were chasing the man were yelling as well, but the suspect would not stop running. Joe yelled out his warning again, "Halt, or I'll shoot." Seeing no reaction, he fired two rapid shots at the fleeing thief. *Blam, blam.* No effect. *Blam, blam.* He fired two more shots and the man went down, hard. His gun skittered across the blacktop. Joe ran over to where he lay, face down, on the pavement.

His fellow officers arrived immediately. Joe still had his gun pointed at the perp, not knowing what to expect next. One of the officers handcuffed the man as he lay face down on the blacktop. Joe rolled him over. The robber was obviously conscious, and he stared at Joe. Joe immediately began to look for the bullet wound but could not find one. He asked him, "Where are you hit?"

The man replied, "I wasn't hit. I fucking tripped, dammit!"

A flood of emotions coursed through Joe's head. He was relieved he hadn't killed the man, and he was happy they had caught him. The adrenaline began to wear off and Joe started to shake. Not wanting his fellow officers to see him trembling, he walked away and let the other officers manhandle the suspect into a squad car.

Joe knew he was justified in shooting at the perpetrator because Illinois had a "fleeing felon law" that allowed police officers to shoot at – wait for it –fleeing felons.

Three weeks later

STONE COTTAGE PUB looks exactly like its name would suggest: Old English architecture featuring lots of stone and lots of dark wood, both inside and out. Officer Joe liked stopping here after working the 4-midnight shift. Usually, when he got off work at 12, he changed into his civilian clothes and headed to the pub. He was frequently hungry at this time and wanted to unwind. The restaurant offered an excellent menu, which for him primarily consisted of pizza, peanuts, and beer. The place had a 2 am license, so he could sit there and relax before driving home. When he was alone, he usually sat at the bar. This allowed him to initiate friendly conversations with his fellow patrons and pass the time in peace.

On this particular Friday evening, or more technically Saturday morning, he sat next to a rather large man with thinning, black, curly hair. To say that the man was hirsute did not fully describe his appearance. The top two buttons on his red plaid shirt were open and his exposed chest looked more like a pelt. His eyebrows did their best to meet in the middle of his forehead and his heavy, though shaven, beard attempted to climb up to his eyeballs. He was the type of man who looked like he needed to shave, even after he just shaved. He wore horn-rimmed, Coke-bottle-thick glasses. If it wasn't for his glasses, he could easily pass for a lumberjack from Maine or Wisconsin. His arms bulged. While he did not have great muscle definition, his arms appeared to be the same size as Joe's thighs. The hair on his arms extended down past the back of his hands and even infested his joints up to the first knuckle. His fingernails were dirty and jaggedly broken rather than clipped. He had a scab on the tip of his nose.

He turned to face Joe and looked at him quizzically. "Do I know you?" he asked.

Joe studied the man's face. "You look familiar. My name's Joe, by the way."

"I'm Jerry. Do you come here a lot?" They shook hands. Jerry's hand completely enveloped Joe's.

"Yeah, a couple of times a month," Joe answered. "What about you? Do you live around here?"

"Not too far," answered Jerry. "Bellwood. Just east of 25th and St. Charles."

"Well, I don't usually go in that direction," Joe replied. "I usually head further out west to Addison."

They both sat silently for a while, studying each other's faces, trying to figure out where they had met. Joe asked, "Where do you work, Jerry?"

Jerry responded, "Well, here and there. It's complicated. What about you?"

"I work right here in Elmhurst."

"What do you do?"

Joe was reluctant to reply. When you tell people you're a cop, they react in funny ways. So, he said, "I work for the village."

Jerry said, "Maybe that's where I've seen you. Do you work in the village hall?"

"Well, sort of," he admitted. "I'm a cop."

Jerry stared at Joe's face and suddenly his eyes flew open wide. "I know you! You're the cop that was shooting at me!"

Joe's jaw dropped. It was one of the few times he could think of absolutely nothing to say.

Jerry said, "I'm so glad you were shooting

over my head!"

Joe sipped his beer and said, "Hell, I wasn't shooting over your head. I was shooting AT you."

Jerry asked, "How the hell did you miss? I ain't exactly a little guy!"

Joe took another swig of his beer. "Yeah, I got a lot of shit about that from the other cops. I even got a nickname – *Bring 'em back alive Joe.*" Both men laughed. Joe looked serious for a moment and then said, "I presume you're out on bail."

"Yeah, yeah. First-time offense, so the bail wasn't too high."

"Well, it was my first time, too," Joe responded. "I've never shot at anybody before. Shooting at someone is a lot different than shooting at a target range," he added, defensively. "All the adrenaline and your heart starts pumping like mad, it makes your hands shake a bit. If you want to know what it feels like, try running a hundred yards as fast as you can, and I fuckin' mean running, not jogging or trotting, but running. That'll get your heart rate up. And then pull out your gun and try to hit the target. And besides, you were moving pretty fast." He went on and asked, "Why did you run? You could have been killed, dummy. In fact, if I was a better shot you would have been."

"I know, I know. I've heard that from everyone." Raising his glass, Jerry said, "Here's to your lack of marksmanship! Let me buy you a beer!"

They both sat there in silence for a few minutes, drinking their beer, eating peanuts, and throwing the shells on the floor. Jerry looked at Joe and asked, "Do you think the Bears will go all the way this year?"

"Hell, yeah! Buddy Ryan has molded together the best defense in the league. Refrigerator Perry's amazing."

Jerry added, "That guy's huge! And when it comes to huge, I know what I'm talking about."

"I love watching 'Sweetness' run."

"Payton's moves, indeed, are a thing of beauty."

And so it went until closing time.

7. Almost Perfect

IT WAS 6:30 in the evening on a beautiful Friday in May and Holly Mueller decided to leave work early. Most of the staff had already left, but the young attorneys like Holly, seeking to impress the partners at the large law firm, typically labored on. She removed her bone-white pumps and put them in her oversized purse. She retrieved her Nike walking shoes and rubbed her feet before putting on a pair of athletic socks that she kept with her shoes.

That's better, she thought as she laced up her Nikes. Holly walked briskly to the elevator, pushed the "down" button, and rapidly descended the twenty-two stories to the polished, white-marble lobby of the prestigious office building on Michigan Avenue. She stepped outside and took a deep breath. It was a beautiful Spring evening and she decided she would walk the mile and a half to her apartment on Oak St. rather than take the bus.

She walked north to the corner, waited for the traffic signal to change, crossed the six lanes of Michigan Ave. to the east side of the street, and turned left to begin her journey home. Having walked this way numerous times in the past, experience taught her that the evening sun would still peek from between the tall buildings and shine on this side of the street. This would make her journey warmer than if she stayed on the shady, west side.

As was her custom, she began to review her day. It was almost perfect. As a recent magna cum laude graduate from Northwestern School of Law, with a specialty in tax law, major legal firms had competed to hire her. She had decided to take a position at Klein, Smith, and McMullen because they had an excellent reputation, offered to help pay off some of her $300,000 student loans, and had a location on Michigan Ave. not that far from her apartment on Oak St. This enabled her to walk home on nice days such as this.

Holly had leased the apartment over three years ago when she had enrolled at Northwestern, because it was only a few blocks from the law school and because it was located very close to the bars and restaurants on Division St. that she enjoyed frequenting along with many other young professionals. She decided she did not need the expense and hassle of a car, or the possibility of a DUI after being "over-served" at one of her favorite night spots.

She was particularly pleased this evening because earlier she had sat in on a late-afternoon meeting with one of the senior partners, Mr. McMullen, and a very important client. She was asked her opinion several times and her answers were spot on. Holly was a bright woman, and she knew it. She was concerned, however, that her appearance may have been the reason for her invitation, rather than her expertise. Mr. McMullen never made a pass at her, nor had he ever touched her, nor even made an untoward remark. Still, the way he sometimes looked at her...

As she stopped at the next intersection to wait for pedestrian traffic to flow again, she looked at herself in the reflection of a storefront window. She was wearing a bone-white, matching skirt and jacket with a bright, red blouse adorned with a small gold necklace and matching earrings. Her mother had once given her a book to read entitled *Dress for Success*. She had politely thanked her mother but never read the book, feeling that everything she needed to learn was covered in the title. At 5'11", Holly knew she was tall for a woman and relatively thin, but with more curves than a professional model. Her shoulder-length, brown, wavy hair and hazel eyes framed her flawless complexion. Long, thin fingers, that would be coveted by all piano players, with beautifully manicured nails completed the package. Throughout her life people had commented on her looks, so she tried to somewhat downplay her attributes, hoping to look more like Mary Ann than Ginger. She wanted to attract men, but not seduce or intimidate them. A difficult balance to achieve.

She decided she was almost perfect. Almost... She didn't smile because her unfortunately crooked teeth were now encased in brand-new braces. She had hoped to get braces as a young teenager rather than waiting until now, but her parents could not afford them. Later, college and law school left her with little discretionary money, so she waited until she started her career. And yes, Klein, Smith, and McMullen offered her dental insurance and yet another reason for choosing to work there.

Lost in her reverie, Holly continued her journey north and was mere blocks away from Chicago's iconic Watertower when her nostrils picked up the scent of something sweet. Her stomach growled. Curious as to what she was smelling, she became more aware of her surroundings, and just up ahead she saw the familiar sign for Garrett's. Her stomach growled again. The aroma was much stronger now. Sweet, yet salty. It beckoned her forward. She was helplessly seduced.

To say that Garrett's sold popcorn would be an oversimplification of their offerings. It would be similar to comparing stale gas station coffee to a frothy Starbucks latte. In the case of Garrett's, the store has a plethora of different types of popcorn, freshly created each day and seasoned with many unique flavors, and frequently combined with other enticing tidbits. This was not your typical movie theater popcorn.

Having lost all self-control, Holly bought a small bag of Pecan Caramel Crisp to comfort her on the rest of her journey home. After leaving the store, she sniffed the bag – *Heaven*! Her mouth watered as she took her first handful of caramel corn and chomped it with delight. *Perfect*. Quickly grabbing another handful, she gleefully bit down.

But in the midst of her joy, her brain signaled "yellow alert." She ignored the warning and once again placed her hand into the bag full of warm caramel-coated popcorn and nuts. And without thinking, gobbled it down as well.

The "yellow alert" in her brain began flashing "RED ALERT." Sirens went off in her head. And pain made its presence felt. Although she had only eaten three handfuls of the sticky, chewy snack, it was three too many. *Oh, crap. My braces. I can't believe I forgot about those things.*

She angrily threw her almost full bag of popcorn into a city trash receptacle and picked up her pace. All of her teeth felt uncomfortable. She knew what it felt like to have something caught between her teeth, but with every tooth involved this was more than twenty-eight times worse. Debris from her snack was lodged everywhere. And the discomfort was mounting with every step she took. Her dental device, cleverly called a "go-between," that was designed to clear her braces of left-over food particles, was carefully left on her bathroom sink. As she walked, Holly began to use her long fingernails to pry the flotsam and jetsam from her mouth, but without being able to see what she was doing she was having little success. She stopped abruptly in front of a window. Using her reflection, she was more easily able to perform her impromptu dental hygiene.

With the removal of each piece, she felt slightly better, so she continued to aggressively stick her fingers in her mouth and poke, prod, and pry. She wanted to rush home, but the relief she was getting from her efforts kept her frozen to the spot. One piece, stuck by the wire of her left rear molar, was particularly troublesome and she had to pull on her cheek with her left hand while her right hand worked to dislodge it. The big globs of caramel that stuck to various protrusions in her dental apparatus had combined with copious amounts of saliva to form strands that joined her top and lower teeth giving her the toothy snarl of Ridley Scott's alien.

While working vigorously on clearing the debris field, she heard a voice to her right yell. "Hey Bucky Beaver, go do your oral surgery somewhere else. You're grossing out my patrons!" She jerked her head and saw an angry, heavy-set Italian-looking man wearing a black tuxedo.

A black tuxedo? He looks like a maitre'd. Oh shit,

he is a maitre'd. But why is he yelling at me? She glanced back at her reflection, her eyes shifted focus, and now she saw through her mirrored image.

To her embarrassment, the window that she was using as a mirror was part of the façade of the new Italian restaurant, *Amalfi*. All the patrons were staring at her as she stood there with her finger buried in her mouth. At the far end of the room, a waiter was pouring wine while a busboy was busy lighting candles and placing them on the white, linen tablecloths. Then as her eyes shifted in focus to the nearest table, she was shocked to see familiar faces. Ms. Smith and Mr. McMullen, two of the three founding partners, and the client she had met only a few hours earlier were sitting at the table looking horrified, their full dinner plates left untouched.

Oh, my God... Maybe they won't recognize me... Oh sure, there are lots of women wearing a white jacket and skirt with a bright red blouse. Shit, they have to know it's me. Her face attempted to turn the same shade of red as her blouse. She didn't know what to do, so she gave a little wave and a curtsy and walked away as rapidly as she could.

I could go home and stick my head in the oven,

except it's electric not gas. Just my luck. But after a while, as she raced toward her apartment, a realization crept in. *Oh well, I always wondered if Mr. McMullen valued my opinion for my mind or merely lusted after my body. If he asks for my opinion after this incident, I'll know he appreciates me for my mind.* And with that, she smiled as best she could with her caramel-coated braces and walked the rest of the way home.

8. Paranoia Strikes Deep

IT WAS 3 am and Jenny woke up. Well, not completely. Her eyes remained screwed tightly shut. But she was aware of her discomfort. She lay absolutely motionless in bed, flat on her back. She felt hot. It was difficult to breathe. There was a pressure on her chest. She was scared.

Oh, shit! COVID-19. It finally got me! Why me?! How the hell did I catch this? I tried to be careful. I planned every excursion so that I could follow the CDC guidelines. I did everything by the book. I've stayed six feet apart from everybody. Baloney! I stayed WAY more the six feet apart from everybody. Even when I went to the store, I wore a mask. Granted, it's not an N-95, but it's still a mask. I even wore motorcycle sunglasses. That extra foam around the eyepiece almost turns them into goggles. I've been wearing them ever since I heard you could get coronavirus through your eyes. I wore the damned gloves. Maybe I touched the outside of the gloves when I took them off. It's hard to take them off without touching the outside. I tried turning them inside out, but sometimes they stick to my hands with all this heat and humidity. I even wore gloves when I filled my car up with gas. Which isn't that often these days. I don't go anywhere. And I wash my hands. I've probably washed them more in the last two months than I have in the last two years.

A "song worm" entered her head. It wasn't the whole song. It never is. It was more of a song fragment. Bob Dylan's nasal twang sang over and over again, "Knock, knock, knockin' on Heaven's door." She never understood what the song was about. It didn't make sense to her. But there was something about that singular phrase of the song that played in the background of every thought she was having.

She reviewed her symptoms.

I'm definitely way hotter than I should be. And I don't run fevers! It can't be a hot flash. I haven't had one of those in years. It's impossible for me to take a deep breath. My chest feels constricted. She coughed a little bit to check her throat. *Yep,* There was a bit of scratchiness there. *I've had that scratchiness for several days, though. I was sure it was seasonal allergies. But now...? Combined with my overheating and difficulty breathing...it's got to be that damn coronavirus.*

Wait a minute! What if it isn't? What if it's only a

heart attack? ... ONLY A HEART ATTACK!? What are the symptoms of a heart attack? I know they're different for women than they are for men. Damn. Everybody knows what the symptoms of a heart attack are for a man. But for a woman...? Why can't I remember? I'm sure shortness of breath is one of them. But a fever? That doesn't make sense. You don't get a fever from a heart attack. So, I was right in the first place. It's probably the coronavirus.

A tear formed in her eye. She still refused to open them. She could feel the warmth of her husband's body next to her. She could hear his rhythmic breathing.

What about Barry? Oh my God! I hope I didn't give it to him. With all of his health issues, he probably won't survive. And if I die and he survives, how will he live? Who will take care of him? .... I wonder if he'll marry someone else. The old adage is that women mourn, men replace. How would he even find someone? How do you meet and date someone and social distance? And at his age I can't picture him hanging out in bars, trying to pick up women. God only knows what he'd be able to with one if he found her.

At least the children are OK. They're grown now and they seem to be doing fine. I wonder if the grandchildren will remember me. The older ones, I'm sure will. But little Barry is only six. My grandfather died when I was six and I have very few memories of him and those are all confused. They're more like brief images than real memories. My God, I don't want to be forgotten!

She sniffled, and another tear formed.

Should I wake Barry? Should I have him take me to the hospital? The news said not to go to the emergency room. They said to call your doctor instead. Right! Like I'll get straight through to my doctor! "Your call is very important to us. If this is a medical emergency, please hang up and dial 9-1-1. Para continuar en Espanol, oprima numero ocho. Please pay attention as our options have changed. Press one for directions to our office. Press two for our hours of operation. Press three if you'd like to make or change an appointment. Press four for prescription services. Press five for instructions on accessing your lab results through your personal portal. Press six to leave a message for the nurse. Press seven if you'd like us to repeat these options. Please leave your name, phone number, and date of birth and we'll get back to you as soon as we're able." SHIT!

I've had a good run. I've had a good marriage. My kids turned out OK. As far as I know, nobody's mad at me. I've seen lots of the world. But there are still so many places to see. What about our cruise to see the ancient marble ruins in the Greek islands next year?!

Hell, without a vaccine that would be turned into a plague ship anyway. Greek Islands? I'll be lucky if I can make it to Coney Island to see the ancient wooden roller coaster!

I've helped a few people. I tried not to hurt people, but I'm sure I did. I made a lot of friends. Oh, damn. They won't even be able to come to my funeral. There'll be nobody to say kind words about me. Oh well, I've always hated funerals anyway.

Her breathing remained strained and try as she might she just couldn't inhale deeply. She was sweating profusely now. A new song worm entered her mind. Frank Sinatra, this time. "And now, the end is near. And so I face the final curtain." She began to sob. For a few moments, all she could think about was that damn song. But then...

Contact tracing. They're going to want to know where I've been and who I've seen in the last two weeks. Hell, I can't even remember what I had for dinner two nights ago. How am I going to trace every place I've been in the last two weeks? I went to Costco. Was that two weeks ago or three? What day did I go grocery shopping? How many packages have I gotten from Amazon? Goddammit! How am I supposed to remember all this shit!?

She tried to sigh but failed.

THE BEST LAID PLANS...

Might as well open my eyes. I can't sleep anyway.

She wiped the tears from her eyes and slowly began to open them. And suddenly, they flew open wide with a start. And that's when she saw him. Her cat, Bailey, sleeping comfortably on her chest. Usually, he sprawled between them at their feet. But tonight, he must have felt particularly lonely, and so he wanted to get "up close and personal." He looked at her, yawned, shifted a little, and went back to sleep.

Bailey was not a sleek Siamese. He was a gold Maine Coon cat who topped the scales at a "wide glide" jumbo-sized twenty-eight pounds. This was a cat who was channeling his fictional mentor, Garfield. Mostly, he ate and slept, with occasional trips to the litter box. His long thick fur provided a thermo-shield from the bedroom's air conditioning. And his two bowling balls of weight had severely restricted her breathing to the point of hypoxia. With some difficulty, she pushed him off her chest. It was very much like pushing a twenty-eight-pound sack of Jell-O that was reluctant to move. As soon as he was off of her body, she took a deep breath and realized she felt much better.

She was so relieved, she began to laugh quietly, for and at herself. She didn't want to wake Barry. She rolled over on her side and a new song worm entered her brain. Buffalo Springfield this time. "Paranoia strikes deep. Into your life it will creep. It starts when you're always afraid..." She improvised the next line. "You step out of line, COVID come and take you away."

9. Rapid Descent: Part I
Damn Girl Scouts!

"Let's go over what you'll need. A bathing suit, a t-shirt to put over the bathing suit, sunscreen, bug repellent, and a sleeping bag, and your usual camping gear. And, oh yeah, gym shoes or sneakers that you don't mind getting wet."

Faye responded, "That's it? Won't I need a life jacket?"

"No," Bart shook his head, "life jackets and paddles are provided."

"Are you sure this is safe?" Faye asked, with her face contorted.

Bart laughed and said, "Sort of. I mean, they take scouts down this river. Of course, we'll be going through a much more challenging section. The easy runs can be a bit boring. A lot of the time you just coast down the river, paddling if you choose, or drifting if you don't. Every once in a while there are Class I or Class II rapids. But we're going down Shotgun Eddy's which is Class

II and III. The real fun comes at the very end when we go over the Big Smokey Falls."

Wait, what?" Faye interrupted. "We're going over a waterfall!?"

"Don't be such a "wuss!" It's not like it's the Niagara. It's a series of steep drops that end in a waterfall and it just kind of shoots you out into a wide, flat part of the river, just like a water slide. It's a real hoot! Just remember, have your life jacket on tight, keep your hands inside of the raft, and do not put your hand on the bottom of the raft. One of my friends, Lynne, did that and broke several of the bones in her hand. Weirdly, her fingers were fine, but all those tendons and bones that lead up to her fingers got badly crunched when her raft landed on a boulder and she had her hand pressed flat on the bottom. The bottom, after all, is just a thin sheet of rubber or neoprene or something like that."

"If you call me a 'wuss' again, when we get to the river, I will hold your head underwater until the bubbles come up."

Bart laughed, "Just teasing. It should be a really good time."

Faye thought for a moment and then asked, "You've done this before, right? And there were no problems?"

"Uhh, I wouldn't say that. Honestly, I almost bought the farm last time. But it wasn't my fault...well, actually, it was totally my fault." Bart stopped talking at this point and had a faraway look on his face.

Faye looked at him intensely, waited a moment, and then demanded, "This is the part where you share the story. It is not the part where you sit quietly and stare off into space."

"OK, OK. You know John DeLongo?" Faye nodded. "He and I were bored and needed to do something to add excitement to our lives. So, we decided to go camping and whitewater rafting in Wisconsin. We chose the Wolf River because it was only five and a half hours north of here. It's north of Shawano and east of Antigo, so it's pretty remote."

Faye interrupted, "I've never heard of either of those towns. It must really be in the boondocks."

Bart explained, "You drive to Green Bay and then head north and a little bit west. We drove up on a Friday night so we could raft on Saturday morning. We chose a long, Class I and II rapids run that would take about seven hours to complete. These are small, two-person rafts, not the ten-person rafts that they have on the Peshtigo River. We figured it would be more fun, just the two of us.

"For some unknown reason, we didn't bring any food, but we cleverly brought a case of beer and stuffed it into a cheap, Styrofoam cooler. Although the rapids are exciting, there are long sections of just slowly drifting in the hot sun. So, naturally, we had a beer. And as we got hotter, we had another. Before too long we realized that most of the beer was gone and we had to pee. Actually, we had to pee several times. And we drank some more.

"The river, for the most part, is very shallow. Not much more than waist-deep. So, we'd hop out of the raft, pee, and climb back in the raft. The river cooled us off, and, as time progressed, we got drunker and drunker. And that's when the trouble began.

"I don't know who was drunker, Johnny, or yours truly, but we were both pretty hammered. We were in a calm part of the river when Johnny decided to paddle really hard, missed the water, and threw his paddle twenty yards behind us. Now, this is bad for a couple of reasons. One, if we lose a paddle, we have to pay an extra $25. And two, it's really hard to maneuver with only one paddle. The river is full of huge boulders. And you use the paddle to push yourself away from the rocks. You're pretty much like a pinball when you're in the rapids, bouncing from rock to rock.

"Being the gallant lad that I am, I jumped out and swam upstream to retrieve the paddle. Then I struggled to catch up with the raft which had kept moving down the river. We were both laughing so hard when I finally caught up with it, I couldn't climb back in. But while we were laughing, the raft continued to pick up speed. I was hanging on to the side of it, and before I knew it, we were in rapids.

"Fortunately, we had life jackets. Unfortunately, they were in the bottom of the raft with the empty beer cooler. I figured I'd be safe if I just hung on to the rope handles laced along the side. But, as I said, the Wolf River is very shallow with a lot of boulders. And we kept banging into rocks, which smashed up my legs. Finally, one big rock hit my leg so hard it ripped my hands free of the raft. Johnny was watching me as I got sucked underwater.

"My whole body was submerged in the current. I twisted myself around so that I was underwater, on my back, moving feet-first down the river. I reasoned that if my feet hit a rock I might survive, but if my head hit a rock, it would scramble whatever brains I had left. I could tell that the river was pushing me along very fast. I could see the surface, only a foot or two above my face, but no matter how hard I tried, I could not reach it. I don't know how long I was underwater, but it was longer than I had ever been submerged before.

"I continued to move like a torpedo just below the surface at high speed. At first, I panicked, but after a while, a strange calm came over me. And I thought to myself, *I've always been afraid of drowning, but this really isn't so bad. In fact, the sunlight hitting all the bubbles in the water from the rapids is quite pretty.* I could hear the roar of the river, but I felt very much at peace. To this day, I don't know if this was caused by the alcohol or the lack of oxygen, but the calmness grew, and slowly things began to fade.

Faye stared at him intently with her mouth open in shock.

"Suddenly, through no conscious effort on my

part, the river spat me upward. My face broke the surface, and I took a big breath of air and that's when the pain set in. My legs hurt, my arms hurt, and I was still in the rapids heading downstream. I knew the rapids would end eventually, but the question in my mind was whether or not I would end before they did. I was swept over a small waterfall with only about a three-foot drop and smashed into some rocks where I got wedged. I was no more than ten feet from the right bank of the river. But I was too sore and weak, and the river was far too strong for me to attempt to cross it.

"I was able to get myself situated so I was fairly secure nestled in the middle of three boulders. I clung there, not knowing what to do. I looked around and could not see far enough up the river to spot any other rafts. I worked very hard to calm myself down. The river was still beating me up, but at least for the moment, I was safe.

"A few minutes later, Johnny, alone in the raft, bounced off the rocks and started past me. He screamed out, 'I'll put ashore as soon as I can and help you. Are you OK?' I was too weak to answer.

"Minutes passed. I could not possibly tell you how many. But, eventually, Johnny showed up, running along the riverbank. He looked frantic and relieved at the same time.

"He yelled over the roar of the river, 'Man, I thought you died! I saw you pulled underwater and you never came up! I was trying to figure out how I would tell your family that you dusted on a rafting trip. I'm so glad to see you. Are you OK?'

"'I guess, but I'm pretty banged up and weak.'

"He pointed out, 'Bart, you only have ten feet to go to get to the shore.'

"'I don't think I can make it. You're going to have to help me.'

"Just then, three Girl Scouts, clad in their uniform tops, got their raft wedged in the rocks directly above me. One of the girls peered down from the front and shouted over the rushing water, 'Hey, there's a man down there!' As she said that, their raft broke free and landed on top of me, pushing my head underwater once again.

"It's amazing what adrenalin can do. I braced my legs on the bottom and roared up to the surface, pushing the raft aside with both my hands. I must have looked like some undersea Godzilla monster as I shoved their raft further down the river.

"Johnny started laughing. 'God, that was awesome. All right, let me find something that you can grab on to'." Johnny left and returned a short time later dragging a tree branch. With one foot in the water, he lifted the branch and pushed it out to me, holding on to his end with both hands. I grabbed it and left the safety of my three rocks as I attempted to walk out of the river. With Johnny pulling on the branch, I was able to cling to it for dear life and struggled to finally make it to shore.

"I lay down because I had no choice. Both of my legs and my left hand were bruised and bleeding. But as I lay there, I realized I could wiggle my toes, move my knees, and it seemed like I lucked out. Nothing was broken. But even though it was probably ninety degrees outside, I began to shake all over, and a wave of nausea swept over me. The nausea and shaking may have been caused by the booze, or they may have been caused by swallowing so much water in the rapids. But my best guess is that it was aftershock from the adrenalin dump I had just received. I went on this trip looking for excitement. And apparently, I far exceeded my quota.

"After I calmed down, and most of the bleeding stopped, I struggled to my feet. We walked along the riverbank to the raft that Johnny had pulled up onto the shore, and from there we could see the M bridge, which was where our trip was scheduled to end."

Faye looked at Bart. "Are you fucking kidding me? This is supposed to make me feel better about rafting? You must have hit your head on one of those rocks!"

Bart stood up and slowly walked around the room. "Look, if you view the story as a cautionary tale on what not to do, we should be fine. Johnny and I screwed up in three ways. We picked the wrong set of rapids to make a run. Seven hours in the broiling sun is too long. We're only going on a three-and-a-half-hour run. But the two biggest mistakes we made were getting drunk and not wearing a lifejacket. I promise you, on my sainted mother's grave, we will not drink until AFTER we are done rafting. And I also promise you, we'll wear our lifejackets on the entire trip."

Faye responded, "From what you've told me, your mother was no saint. And isn't she still alive?"

"OK, OK. But we will wear lifejackets and we will not drink. If we follow those rules, we'll be fine. What could possibly go wrong?"

10. Rapid Descent: Part II
What Could Possibly Go Wrong?

"Knock, knock."

"Really? C'mon Bart!"

"Play along! Knock, knock."

"Alright, alright! Who's there?"

"Dwayne."

Faye let out a big sigh. "Dwayne who?"

Bart smiled and said, "Dwayne the tub, I'm dwonding!"

"I tell you, Bart, I could hit you with this paddle. Throw you in the river and no one would ever know. And seeing you have no friends, no one would ever care."

Bart began laughing at his own joke and Faye's annoyance.

With an exasperated look, Faye asked, "You tell a lot of jokes, don't you Bart. Why?"

"A lot of times I tell jokes just to amuse myself. You know, in schools they tell teachers to ignore bad behavior and reinforce good behavior.

That didn't work so well with me. I was always self-reinforcing. I cracked myself up. And the teacher's reaction was beside the point. I also tell jokes whenever I'm feeling almost any strong emotion. It's really hard to be depressed while you're laughing. Some people cry when they're stressed. Some scream and swear. Me, I tell jokes. Probably to keep from crying, screaming, and swearing."

"Does it work?"

"Yeah, most of the time. But sometimes I'll revert to screaming and swearing. I got that from my mother."

"Look, if I promise to give you a cookie, will you promise not to tell any more jokes?"

"Hmmm…what kind of cookie?"

"They're chocolate cookies with macadamia nuts. I made them myself."

In an overly dramatic, theatrical motion, Bart wiped the imaginary saliva from his mouth and did his best Cookie monster impression. "Cookie…me want cookie. Me make deal!" he proclaimed.

"Pinkie swear?"

"What am I, an eight-year-old girl?"

"Pinkie swear?"

"OK, OK," he said as they interlocked their little fingers.

Bart and Faye were sharing a gray, two-person raft as they gently drifted down the Wolf River in Wisconsin. It was early afternoon on a beautiful August day. The river, at this point, was moving steadily toward the Big Smokey Falls. Dense forest lined both shores and occasional boulders were scattered haphazardly in the river creating eddies in the current. The water was brown but clear enough to see the six feet to the rocky bottom. They sat facing each other on two wooden benches that were stretched across the tubes of the raft. Bart sat in the rear seat with Faye sitting in front. She was facing backward so she could talk with Bart. Both wore their bright, orange lifejackets.

"These cookies are the cat's meow," said Bart.

"Meow!" Faye purred. "There's no combination like chocolate and macadamia nuts. And the Diet Coke pairs well with both. Even if it is a conflict in dietary philosophies." After pausing for another sip of Diet Coke, Faye continued, "Do you know what I miss, Bart?"

"No, what?"

"I miss Fresca."

"You miss what?"

"You know, Fresca. One of the first diet sodas."

"You actually liked that? My God, I thought I was the one supposed to tell jokes. You know, I spilled some of that on my table and the cat tried to bury it."

"C'mon. It wasn't that bad."

"Allow me to retort. Oh yes, it was."

"It was nice and grapefruity. I like grapefruity!"

"I've got a whole bunch of jokes for that."

"Bart, you promised. No more jokes. By the way, shouldn't we be paddling or something?"

"Well, we can if you want to. But I prefer to just drift. We're not renting the raft by the hour. And we'll be at the pick-up point long before closing."

"Ouch!"

Bart asked, "What happened?"

"That damned fly bit me! Hey, there's another one." In a matter of moments, they were surrounded by a swarm of deer flies. They were shooing them off themselves and each other as they slowly drifted down the river. Faye spun around on her seat to face forward, grabbed her paddle, and said, "Uh...maybe we should start paddling now to see if we can get away from them."

"Sounds like a plan to me."

They ferociously paddled, but deer flies are among the fastest insects in the world and had little difficulty keeping up with them. But after about five minutes, the deer flies disappeared as quickly as they arrived.

"Do you hear that?" Faye pivoted once again in her front seat.

"Yeah, I think we're getting close to the falls. The river is kind of high right now. This area has had a lot of rain."

Faye looked at him and said, "I don't mind telling you, I'm a little scared of this."

"Well, that's because you're intelligent. If you were stupid, going over the falls wouldn't bother you. To tell the truth, I'm a little nervous, too. When I was at the camp store, I heard the owner talking. Apparently, a guy got killed here last year going over the falls."

"And you waited until now to tell me this?"

"Look, make sure your lifejacket is on tight. Don't try to paddle in the falls. Just lay your paddle down in the bottom of the raft and hang on. Pull the bottom strap on your lifejacket tighter." Bart pointed to hers and then pulled his tighter. Bart smiled and said, "You probably don't want to pull the top strap too tight. You don't want to squish 'the girls.'"

"Bart, I swear, I'm going to kill you."

They were picking up speed now. Faye pivoted to face forward and both she and Bart placed their paddles on the bottom of the raft. They held so tightly to the lines along the side that their knuckles turned white. They couldn't see the falls, but they could definitely hear them roaring now. The ordinarily broad river got narrower and narrower as it approached a funnel-like gap between two slabs of granite. The river usually appeared level, but now Faye and Bart had the distinct impression that they were going downhill. They continued to accelerate. The river, which was mostly clear and brown like tea, now turned pure white with foam and bubbles. As they rounded a sharp turn to the left, the roar became deafening. There was a flash of white as the water slapped them in the face and blinded them. Their stomachs lurched as the raft careened over the edge of the falls and shot forward. And then all was calm.

Faye's hair covered her eyes. Every square inch of her was soaked. The lifejacket that she had so carefully tightened was now pushed up to her ears by the force of the water. She pulled it down as she brushed the hair from her face and wiped the water from her eyes. She had been holding her breath as they plummeted over the falls and now sucked in air greedily and squealed with delight. "That was awesome! Just like the log ride at Great America, only ten times more fun! What a blast!" Laughing, she turned around to face Bart and saw only an empty seat.

★ ★ ★

MEANWHILE, BART LOOKED up at the waterfall. He could see it, but somehow it looked wrong. And the sound. The sound was a different pitch than what it should have been. He stared at the waterfall. It seemed that he was looking through crinkly cellophane. *What the...?* he thought. It was at that point that he realized he was on the bottom of the river, looking up at the falls from underwater.

★ ★ ★

ALONE IN THE raft, Faye became frantic, looking desperately in every direction, searching for Bart in the water. She was screaming out his name.

★ ★ ★

BART, IN THE meantime, was quite perplexed as he sat on the bottom of the river. *Shit*, he thought, *I've been thrown out of the raft. But at least this time I have my trusty lifejacket on.* And with that, he reassuringly patted his chest to feel his lifejacket. It was gone.

★ ★ ★

AS FAYE FRANTICALLY swiveled in her seat, trying to figure out what happened, an empty, bright orange lifejacket popped to the surface. She screamed.

★ ★ ★

ALTHOUGH ONLY A few seconds had passed, it dawned on Bart that he needed air. So, he tucked his legs under him and pushed as hard as he could to the surface. The water there was only about six feet deep and he launched out of the river doing a great impression of Shamu at Sea World. He heard Faye screaming before he saw her. He realized that all of his parts worked perfectly well, and he was unhurt. So, he calmly side-stroked his way to the raft.

"You fucking jerk! You scared me half to death. How could you do that to me?"

"Do what?"

"Jump out of the raft like that you moron. You and your fucking jokes."

"Faye, I didn't jump out of the raft. I got thrown out of the raft. Why are you mad at me? I wasn't joking around. I could have drowned."

"You're such a clown, I never know when you're being serious or joking."

As Bart climbed awkwardly into the raft, he looked at her and said, "Faye, you know me. Do you really think I'm coordinated enough to do a swan dive out of a raft going over a waterfall while taking off my lifejacket? And not break anything? There were only two chances I could pull that off. Slim and none. And Slim just left town."

Faye smacked him on the back of the head. "Always with the jokes. This is why I can't take you seriously."

All of her excitement, fear, anger, and relief exploded at once and Faye started to cry. Bart leaned forward and hugged her. As her sobs subsided, she pulled back slightly and wiped her nose with the back of her hand. Looking at her hand with disgust, she leaned over the side of the raft and rinsed it in the river.

"You know, Faye, I really thought everything would be fine if we wore our lifejackets and didn't drink."

She sighed heavily, then took a deep breath trying to regain control. "Guess we'd better pick up your lifejacket. You don't want to lose your five-dollar deposit."

"Wait, what? I gave up drinking on this trip for a lousy five dollars? I need a beer!"

"Me too, Bart! Me too!"

11. The Little Ninja that Could

BRETT AND JIM stood talking at the side of the secretary's desk. Brett was the special education director for the behavior disordered program at Jack London High School. The irony of having a behavior disordered program (commonly referred to as BD) at a school named after the author of *Call of the Wild* never ceased to amuse him. Jim was a special education teacher whose areas of expertise included English, History, and gossip.

The special education resource room served several functions. In the corner, directly across from the door, was a small, wood-paneled office for the director, Brett, although he typically spent little time there. The secretary's desk was located immediately to the left of the entrance, about six feet away from Brett's office. Scattered throughout the large room were desks for the teachers to use as they prepared lessons and assisted students. The rest of the room housed workstations that were occupied each period by students who were coming to work on assignments or get help from the special education resource teachers and aides.

It was 1978, and the revolutionary Public Law 94-142 had just taken effect. This law required that students with "special needs" be given an "appropriate" education in the "least restrictive environment," and penalties such as expulsion for students with disabilities would become a remedy of the past. To accommodate the new law, special education programs were set up in public schools all over the country. And because these programs were new and few administrators liked behavior disordered students, such programs were typically stuffed into the corner of the attic or the basement of older schools. Basically, out of sight, out of mind.

Jack London's program was located in the basement next to an extremely large study hall. Both rooms were painted a pale yellow in a feeble attempt at mimicking sunlight shining into them. The resource room had a surprising number of windows that looked directly at a dirty, gray cement wall only four feet away. Twelve-inch pipes, wrapped in asbestos, jutted up from the floor to the ceiling of both rooms on their journey from the nearby boiler room to radiators on the first and second floors of the school. Over the past few months, students had stabbed the asbestos with their pens and fingernails and pulled chunks of it off the pipes. Small bits of white, chalky asbestos lay scattered around at the base of the pipes, waiting to be swept up each night by the janitors.

The study hall filled gaps in student's schedules, and most periods contained approximately 125 students who were all very busy not studying. The rows and aisles of desks lined up in a rectangular formation that would have done the Army Corps of Engineers proud. The only entrance to the special education room ran through this study hall.

Brett asked Jim, "What do you think of our new teacher?"

Jim replied, "Well, she sure is cute. And she sure is tiny. I'm not convinced she's tough enough to handle our budding Mafiosos."

The new teacher they were discussing, Cathy Ohara was, indeed, a petite, young woman of Japanese ancestry. She stood barely five-foot-tall, and when her long black hair, which reached all the way down to her lower back, was soaking wet, she tipped the scales at a whopping ninety-five pounds.

RJ, short for Roberta Jackson, the secretary, chimed in. "I have my reservations about her as well. She's so young and she looks fragile. And this is her first high school job. She's got a great sense of humor, though."

Brett looked at her and responded, "Oh?"

"She was dealing with a book vendor on the speakerphone, and he said something like, 'Cathy Ohara. I can see those Irish eyes smiling now.' Cathy responded, 'Boy have you got that wrong! My family were rice growers, not potato farmers'."

Jim smiled and took a sip of his cold coffee and said, "I'm glad she has a sense of humor. My concern is, is she tough enough. Hell, even the freshman boys are taller than she is."

Brett stroked his beard. "I guess we'll just have to see how she reacts to one of our charm-school dropouts."

At that moment, the door to the special-ed room opened. Cathy and a sophomore boy, who was at least a foot taller than she was, were having a vigorous disagreement as they entered from the study hall. The boy, Angelo DeTomasso, had a bad temper and a short fuse. Angelo was justifying his lack of progress in his English class by blaming the teacher. Cathy responded calmly, "I understand your difficulties, but we're here to help. All you need to do is ask."

Angelo continued spewing out excuse after excuse and winding himself up to the inevitable explosion. Brett, Jim, and RJ just watched. Cathy was using the "broken record" method, designed to wear down resistance. She responded, "I understand that you're having difficulties. But when you're having difficulties, all you have to do is ask for our help."

Angelo was definitely not getting the responses he wanted and got louder and louder. It appeared that he wanted to show her that he was in charge and felt that if he could force her to react in fear, he would "own her" for the rest of the year. He towered over her, hoping to intimidate her with his height. She stood calmly, maintaining eye contact, and said, "Angelo, I understand you are getting upset. But when you need help, all you need to do is ask for it."

Jim moved to intervene, but Brett reached out his arm and held him back. He whispered to Jim,

"If we intervene now, she'll lose face. Let's see how she handles this."

At this point, Angelo blew up. He opened the door to the study hall and screamed, "I've had it with you, you fucking little whore!" He then kicked over an empty desk and ran up the stairs and down the hall.

All 125 students in the study hall became dead silent and stared at Cathy who stood in the doorway. Brett, Jim, and RJ as well as several special education students and aides who were located in the resource room all stopped what they were doing as well and stared.

Cathy, realizing she was the center of attention, quietly closed the door to the study hall and, in a great show of fake indignation, stamped her foot and declared, "I am not that little!" And after a brief pause, she added softly to the three nearby staff members, "Fucking whore! Isn't that redundant?"

Brett turned to Jim and said, "That's the best case of deflection I've ever heard."

RJ laughingly added, "Cathy, I think you're upset about the wrong parts of Angelo's accusation."

Cathy shrugged her shoulders and calmly

walked to her desk.

Jim smiled and said, "I think that little Ninja will do just fine!"

12. A Cat in a Tree

"You're late!"

"I know, I know. I'm sorry."

"And you're out of uniform. What's with the light blue shirt? It's supposed to be white."

"I'm sorry, boss, but I really have a good excuse. My cat…"

"Wait a minute! You're not going to tell me some lame ass excuse about how your cat ate your homework – or in this case, your white shirt!"

Bonnie was a thin woman in her mid-fifties. Her wavy brown hair showed not a hint of gray, most likely due to her love affair with Clairol. She was dressed in the white shirt and black pants that are required by Delancey's restaurant. She stood with her hands on her hips and spoke with an aggravated tone in her voice. She was a bright and cynical woman who did not take kindly to any excuse for poor performance. At the moment, she was interrogating her long-term employee,

Anthony.

Delancey's is a small restaurant in the Hollywood area of Los Angeles very near the Nickelodeon sound stage. The restaurant is housed in a brick building located on the corner of Sunset Blvd. and Tamarind Ave. Delancey's chief claim to fame is that it is not famous at all. Consequently, its customers include many television and movie stars who are filming nearby. It is a convenient place to meet with their friends and family after work. They appreciate being able to eat in peace without being bothered by tourists begging for autographs and selfies.

Bonnie looked him in the eye and said, "Anthony, let's go in the back. I don't want the patrons to hear, and we have a few minutes before the dinner rush comes in. I can't wait to hear your cat story."

Anthony followed her, and his face broke into a crooked smile that was both endearing and annoying, depending upon the viewer's mood at the moment. Although he stood at only 5' 8", he walked with a poise and grace that exuded self-confidence. They sat in the far back booth next to the glassed-in wine storage room.

"All right, Anthony, tell me a cat story. Does it

involve Barbara Streisand singing *Memories*?"

"OK, OK. You know I have a cat named Gizmo, right?"

Bonnie nodded.

"Well, Gizmo has been missing for two days now, and my wife has been very upset. So, shortly before I came to work, I decided I would walk the neighborhood. I was looking to see if perhaps he had been hit by a car and was lying in the gutter somewhere, but I didn't want to tell her that so I told her I was going to see if I could find him. I left the house calling his name, more for her benefit than anything else, because, unlike dogs, cats don't come when they're called unless it involves calling them for dinner. And even then, it's iffy.

"I walked around the block, still calling his name. And wouldn't you know it, I heard him meow. At first, I couldn't figure out where he was calling from, but then I looked up and saw him near the top of a twenty-foot tree. I kept calling for him to come down, but he just stayed there and yowled at me. I rushed back home to tell my wife that I found Gizmo and that he was fine, just up at the top of a tree. She glared at me and, in a not-so-friendly tone, asked why I didn't get him down.

"Realizing I had to get to work, I brushed it off and sang, *'I'm not a lumberjack, but I'm OK.* The cat will come down when he's ready.' But as I was putting on my white shirt for work, she looked up *Cats in a Tree* on the internet and found that if a cat climbs up a tree and can't get down, they can become dehydrated, lose consciousness, and fall out of the tree to their death. Apparently, cats have an easy time climbing up a tree, but not getting down. Ordinarily, if a cat is conscious, it will be able to take a fall very easily. But an unconscious cat may plummet to the earth headfirst and do a face plant. Now my wife was more upset than ever.

"The cat had been gone for two days, and she demanded that I do something immediately. I had a five-foot step ladder for work around the house, but that simply wasn't going to cut it."

Bonnie twirled her index finger pointing to the ceiling, indicating that Anthony should speed it up. She was obviously losing her patience.

"I know you're upset with me, boss, but I'd rather deal with you than my wife. The most you can do is fire me. But she can make my life miserable for the rest of my days. So, back I went to the tree with no plan in mind.

"I got to the tree and kept calling up to Gizmo, but all he would do was to yowl back down to me. It seemed to me like he was scared. I hoped I could wait him out and he would finally come down, but I remembered an old adage by Robert Heinlein – never try to out-stubborn a cat. It became painfully obvious that waiting wouldn't work, but I could see no way that I could climb the tree. And even if I could, how would I get down holding a cat?

"I paced around the tree trying to figure out what to do when I noticed a long extension ladder next to one of the neighboring houses. Hoping to borrow the ladder, I hustled up the two steps and rang the doorbell. A short, elderly, dark-complected man opened the door, and I immediately began to explain my situation. He held up his hand and called out '*Maria! Ven aca!*' So, someone I supposed was Maria came to the door. She was about ten years old and apparently acted as the designated family translator."

Bonnie interrupted. "So, your nickname is Tony and you just met a girl named Maria?"

"Good one, boss!" Anthony replied with a grimace and then continued with his story,

"Anyway, I explained that I wanted to borrow the ladder to rescue my cat. She translated for her grandfather, and he motioned toward the ladder and shook his head 'yes.' At that point, my two years of D-level high school Spanish kicked in, and I said, 'Gracias.' Hey, it's so easy when you know the language!"

Bonnie grimaced.

"The old man and his granddaughter stepped out of the house and watched as I grabbed the ladder and leaned it up against the tree. I extended it as far as it would go, and it ended up just below Gizmo. I shakily climbed on to the ladder and made my way higher and higher. (By the way, did I mention I'm afraid of heights? Hell, I don't even like being this tall!) But I'm more afraid of my wife than heights, so I figured my odds of surviving were better with the ladder than with her. Meanwhile, the old man and his granddaughter watched intently from their front stoop, pointing towards the cat.

"Now, nobody can say I don't love an audience. Even so, I was not expecting one. A young couple walking hand in hand stopped in mid-stride to see what Grandpa was pointing at and stared at me precariously climbing the ladder. A

CAPTAIN BILLY C.

jogger came to a halt to join the couple staring up into the tree as he continued to jog in place. A mailman, wearing his ever-so-stylish Bermuda shorts, stopped as well. Apparently 'neither snow nor rain nor heat nor gloom of night stays these couriers from the swift completion of their appointed rounds,' but a cat stuck in a tree will. Other people stopped as well, some standing in their front yards, some gaping at me from the sidewalk.

"As I climbed the ladder, the cat seemed to become more and more agitated. When I got near the top, I was still too low. But then I figured that if I climbed up near the very top of the ladder, you know, the place you're not supposed to stand, and hung on to a branch with my right hand, I could stretch out my left hand and just reach the cat. I could hear the crowd gasp. What I didn't count on was how scared and excited Gizmo was. Because as I grabbed him and began to pull him toward me, he peed. The pee landed on the side of my forehead as I was looking up. It ran down my cheek, just missing my eye and mouth. More of it ran down my left arm to my armpit. It's amazing how much urine a ten-pound cat can hold. But I managed to pull Gizmo to my chest and slowly, with only one arm to assist me, sloshed my way down the ladder. My audience at first broke into applause when I reached the cat, but then as the cat began to relieve itself, I heard an audible gasp that was quickly replaced by gales of laughter as the crowd slowly dispersed, leaving only Grandpa and Maria."

Anthony looked at Bonnie expectantly, waiting for some sort of reaction. Bonnie stared at him with a wry smile and said nothing. Not getting the response he had hoped for, he continued.

"Cats are very particular about where they pee, and almost never pee from a tree. So, Gizmo probably hadn't peed for two days. And because he hadn't had anything to drink since climbing the tree two days ago, he was dehydrated. Consequently, this pee was so concentrated and toxic that it could have been banned by the Geneva Convention. I mean, just one whiff could cause 'dain bramage.'"

Bonnie groaned.

"By the way," Anthony went on, "did you know that laughter in Spanish sounds the same as laughter in English? Grandpa and Maria, of course, were laughing hysterically as my urine-covered carcass descended the ladder. By the time

CAPTAIN BILLY C.

I got down, they were holding their stomachs, doubled over with laughter. Do you know how hard it is to look dignified with cat urine running down your face and arm? As I ran home with Gizmo in my arms, leaving a vapor trail, I could still hear the laughter echoing behind me.

"So, boss, I couldn't come to work smelling like cat piss, right? And all my other white shirts were in the laundry. So, the only thing I could do was take a quick shower and wear this blue one. And now I'm here."

Bonnie sighed. "And now you're here." She was silent for a moment, lost in thought. She looked at him and said, "Anthony, I've got a couple of questions. You, like every other waiter in this place, are either hoping to star in a movie or write a screenplay. If I recall correctly, you're trying to do both."

"Yeah, boss, I'm trying. But what's your point?"

"Like most people here, I've tried to become a screen writer myself. And if memory serves me correctly, there's a writing assignment for budding novelists and playwrights that involves a cat in a tree. You'll have to correct me if I'm wrong, but the assignment is to describe rescuing a cat in a tree, making sure to include that there is a problem with a simple rescue. You know, the cat's in a tree, and I try to save it, but the first plan won't work. The second plan looks like it's going to work, but unforeseen difficulties arise that make that plan fail. And only through clever thinking, a third plan proves successful. Sometimes with unintended consequences. Is that about right, Anthony?"

"Uhh, yeah boss. But this really did happen," Anthony said in his most sincere voice.

"Hey, Anthony, you're a pretty good actor too, am I correct?"

"I like to think so, boss, but..."

"Hmmmmm..." Bonnie took a deep breath and exhaled slowly. With an exasperated sigh, she said, "Just get back to work."

Anthony rose from the booth and headed to the front of the restaurant. He turned. "It's a true story, boss," he said with a hurt look on his face.

Bonnie ignored his pitiful expression, "On-time tomorrow, right? And with a white shirt!"

13. Romance on the Beach: Part I
A Three-Hour Tour

CONNIE LOOKED AT her new boyfriend and said, "Blake, we need to talk."

Blake got that pained look on his face that all males experience when an important woman in their life says, "we need to talk." He replied, "Ooohhhhh K...." and sat down on the couch next to her.

"Honey, we've been dating now for several months. And don't get me wrong, I'm really enjoying our relationship."

Blake added, "But..."

"Well, I think we need to move on to the next level."

"Woah, you want to get married?" Blake raised his hands in a self-defensive posture and displayed a melodramatically shocked expression.

"Of course not, you idiot." She paused. "Like I said, we've been dating for several months..."

Blake interrupted, "Four months, six days, and," he looked at his watch, "seventeen hours and twelve minutes."

"You made that up, you clown! Are you going to listen to me or not?"

"Sheesh! I'm sorry. It's just that when you tell me we need to talk, it scares the hell out of me. Please continue, and I won't interrupt."

"Anyway, I said we should take things to the next level. And for me, that means taking a trip together."

Blake couldn't help himself and responded, "Oh, thank God! For a minute I thought you wanted to get married, or were expecting a baby, or were wanting to get a puppy, or were expecting a puppy. Compared to that, a trip's no big deal."

"Blake, I'm being serious. A trip is a big deal. We get along fine when we go out to dinner, see a movie, and even when we work together. But a trip presents its own set of difficulties. We haven't been put under the test of stress, yet. And I don't know how we'll react to each other when things don't go as planned. And a vacation together is just the thing to test our relationship. If we still get along and we haven't killed each other by the

CAPTAIN BILLY C.

time we get back, I'll feel better about us and our future."

"Hey, I'm up for it if you are. Where do you want to go?"

"It was my idea to take a vacation together. So, I think it's only fair if you pick the location."

"Hmmm, is this part of the test too?" Blake asked suspiciously.

"Of course! I hope you pick well!"

"In that case, I've got a great idea for some international travel."

"That sounds intriguing. Go on."

"We can go to the International Hockey Hall of Fame in Toronto."

"Wait a minute! You want to go to Toronto, to the Hockey Hall of Fame, in March when the weather is oh-so-pleasant in Canada?"

"Well, you said it was my choice."

"BLAKE...!"

"OK. OK, I'll settle for my second choice. How about if we fly to Miami, rent a car, and drive down to the Florida Keys? You told me you always love beaches, and I think we're both tired of the gray skies of Chicago in winter. A little sunshine will do us both good. Of course, you realize I'm giving up my lifelong dream to see

Stan Mikita's hockey puck just to go to the beach with you!"

"You know Blake, people have asked me if I have a child. And I always tell them, 'just my boyfriend.'"

April 1, 1980 – Key Largo, FL

"Can we go?" Connie asked excitedly.

"I suppose. If they have room for us."

Connie was intrigued by the possibility of going on a glass-bottomed boat to look at the reef off Key Largo. Blake made a sharp left turn into the parking lot where the boat was docked. The sign on the ticket booth said that the tour left at one o'clock. It was ten to one, so they ran up to the window and were lucky enough to purchase tickets.

As they walked toward the dock, Blake looked at the boat. It wasn't very long – around fifty to sixty feet. But it was fairly wide. The water was so clear he could see that the boat had a shallow draft with windows lining both the port and starboard sides underwater. The American flag at the stern stood straight out in the wind.

A bit breezy, he thought.

CAPTAIN BILLY C.

Connie clutched his right hand as they walked the gangplank to board. "I'm really looking forward to this," she exclaimed. "The guidebook said there were hundreds of types of fish living on the reef. I feel like I'm Jacques Cousteau. Thank you for stopping here. This is going to be wonderful."

Blake turned and looked at the flag at the stern again. *Definitely breezy*, he thought. They made their way onto the boat and found two of the few empty seats along the port side. It was going to be a crowded trip.

The boat cast off without incident, and a pre-recorded safety message was broadcast on the intercom. All this was very standard. But then, a female crewmember got on the loudspeaker and said, "Hello, and welcome aboard. My name is Melody and I'm here to help you have the most comfortable trip possible. I'd like to invite you to come to the snack bar at the bow of the boat – that's the pointy end for you landlubbers – where we have a variety of snacks and beverages available for purchase. In addition, we will be happy to give you, free of charge, Dramamine tablets." Her voice began to take on a pleading tone, "You need to take them now, so you don't get seasick. It takes at least a half-hour for the pills to take effect, so please, please come up to the bow now. It's rough out on the reef. If you wait until we get to the reef it will be too late to take them then." She paused for a moment and then continued, "And now for our schedule. It takes a half-hour to forty-five minutes to get to the reef and about the same to get back. We'll spend about an hour and a half on the reef. And that is the itinerary for our three-hour tour."

Melody resumed pleading for another few minutes for the passengers to take Dramamine as the boat picked up speed. After clearing the channel, the ship's speakers came back on, this time playing nautical-themed music. First came Jimmy Buffet's *Cheeseburger in Paradise* followed by Gordon Lightfoot crooning the *Wreck of the Edmund Fitzgerald*. Connie and Blake looked at each other. Blake exclaimed, "Wow, that's an interesting choice of music for a boat trip on a windy day!"

After a moment, Connie's face grew quizzical and she asked Blake, "What was all that stuff about taking Dramamine?"

"I don't know. I've been on lots of boats before, but I have never heard a crewmember offer to pass out Dramamine before the trip even got going. Maybe we should take some,"

Connie thought for a moment and replied, "I don't think so. I'm not sure I want to take a pill given to me by a boat crew member. And anyway, Dramamine makes me sleepy. I don't want to get out to the reef and fall asleep. I really want to see the fish."

"Well, I've never been seasick," Blake said with an air of confidence that he didn't really feel. "So, I guess I'll pass on the Dramamine also."

Connie's long, auburn hair was streaming out behind her as the boat picked up speed. She pulled a Scrunchie out of her purse and struggled to get her hair all in one place so she could put it in a ponytail. She was afraid that her hair would be slapping the faces of the passengers sitting behind her.

After securing her hair, she said, "I don't think I'll feel seasick at all. This boat is smooth enough." She didn't realize that the mangrove trees and small islands were smoothing out the water and that the pitching of the boat was ameliorated by the fact that it was speeding "on plane," and consequently less subject to the swells. People lined up three deep to purchase various food items at the snack bar. But Blake noticed very few took up the offer for free Dramamine.

After about forty minutes, the boat began to slow. The captain steered the boat to a mooring ball while the crew scrambled forward and secured the bow to a mooring cable. Once secured, Melody, who was advising everyone to take Dramamine earlier, once again broadcast on the loudspeakers. "Please be careful as you take the stairs down to the bottom of the boat to look out the windows and see our beautiful reef in John Pennekamp State Park."

Connie and Blake made their way to the bottom of the boat where the large windows on the port and starboard side looked out and down on the reef. There were several benches along the keel of the boat allowing people to sit and stare out the windows. Children ran up to the glass and pressed their faces against it, blocking the view of everyone else in the boat, as parents tried, unsuccessfully, to wrangle their children to their seats so everyone could see. The passengers jabbered excitedly to each other.

"Look there's an eel!"

"I see an angelfish."

CAPTAIN BILLY C.

"What's that bright, blue fish called?"

As more and more people stuffed themselves into the compartment, the air grew uncomfortably warm and stale. The boat began to rock. And the mass of people gasped in unison. Connie gave a startled glance to Blake.

The motion of a ship that is moored in high winds falls into several categories. As the ocean swells hit the boat it rises and falls, rises and falls. But that is not all that happens. Because of the wind, this rising and falling is also met by pitching, which is a teeter-totter-like motion. This means that the bow of the boat rises and the stern plummets until the wave passes by. Then the bow plummets and the stern rises. But then a third motion strives to destroy your equilibrium. The boat will roll from side to side. Starboard side down, port side up. And then the reverse. All three motions, rising and falling, pitching (bow to stern), and rolling (starboard to port) are independent of each other. Consequently, there is little to no predictability as to what movement the passengers will feel. One moment they are staring almost straight down to the bottom of the reef and then they are pitched high enough to see the sky. And to make matters worse, because the wind was variable, the boat began to swing on the mooring. Sometimes it was facing east, then north, then east, and finally south.

Even while seated, passengers had to brace their feet and hold on to the benches to keep from tumbling into the side of the boat windows and each other. For some, a sudden epiphany arrived. "Boy, a second trip to the snack bar may not have been the wisest of choices."

The tall blond lady who worked the snack bar and the public address system wheeled a large 50-gallon blue plastic barrel to the back end of the viewing area. The inside of the barrel was protected by a huge black garbage can liner. She shook her head and walked away in dismay.

It's hard to say who was first. But someone ran to the barrel, bent their head over, and began retching violently into the can. Because the room had so little ventilation, and the air was already stale, the fresh smell of vomit permeated everyone's nostrils almost instantaneously. And since the engines were off while moored, the retching sound echoed in the enclosed space. It wasn't long before several more people were gathered around in a circle, throwing up their ill-advised snacks.

Connie looked at Blake and said, "Oh God!" and muscled her way between two big men to the vomit can herself. He noticed that her beautiful tan had taken on a slight green tinge.

More and more people surrounded the garbage can, short people like Connie in the front, and taller people throwing up over their shoulders. Blake raced to stand behind Connie. He held her hair so it wouldn't droop down in front of her face where it risked being "vomitized" by her or one of her new companions-in-spew. He held her hair at arm's length and looked away as more and more people clamored toward the can. Although he was nauseous, he managed to keep his breakfast down by looking toward the windows at the bottom of the boat.

With the crowd completely blocking access to the barrel, a second wave of nauseous passengers raced up the stairway, hoping the fresh air would save them. It didn't. They bent over the railings and began to vomit on both sides of the ship. The smart or lucky ones settled on the leeward side of the boat as opposed to the windward, thus avoiding the blowback of the windward side.

Unaware of the commotion above-deck, Blake continued to stare out the underwater windows when he saw partially digested bits of food slowly drifting down towards the reef. The beautiful fish that had so enchanted everybody earlier viewed it as manna from heaven and began to delightedly pick over the previously eaten food. More and more fish arrived, and a vomit-fueled feeding frenzy ensued.

Blake grew nauseous, and he felt he could no longer stay in the viewing compartment, aka. Roman-style vomitorium. He handed Connie her hair and said, "I have to get out of here." She grunted in response, stuffed her hair down the front of her t-shirt, and proceeded to hurl once again.

Blake staggered his way up the stairs to the main deck. He found an empty chair and table and sat there, staring at the horizon while white-knuckling the table's surface. That's when he saw a chubby, freckle-faced ten-year-old boy in a bright red shirt who was absolutely delighted with the unscheduled festivities. He held a bag of Cheetos and would walk up to people who were not throwing up, stand in front of them, and proceed to eat each Cheeto slowly, with his orange-colored mouth wide open. He laughed hysterically when that person bolted from their seat and raced up to the railing to add another fish-friendly feast.

The boy spotted Blake and figured he'd found his next victim. He ran up to him, but before he could begin his slow chewing, Blake looked him in the eye and said, "Get away from me you little bastard or I'll rip out your fucking heart." The boy realized that Blake just might be serious, so he left abruptly looking for easier targets to victimize.

Several of the passengers who could retch no more started asking the captain to take them back to port. The captain said, "I'm contracted to spend an hour and a half on the mooring."

At this point more passengers gathered around and demanded that the captain leave, screaming things like, "We don't care about your contract, get us the hell out of here!"

After a few brief moments of silent reflection, the captain decided he didn't want to star in a 1990 version of *Mutiny on the Bounty*. After all, he reasoned, discretion is the better part of valor. He ordered the engines to be started and the crew to cast off the mooring line. Several of the people cheered, others wept, and a few kept on vomiting. As the boat picked up speed, the smell of vomit slowly was left behind. Blake imagined the fish waving goodbye and saying, "Thanks for lunch." He smiled to himself, as best as he could, given the circumstances.

After the boat docked, people staggered as rapidly as they could to get to dry land. Blake and Connie only managed to get a few yards onto the lawn before collapsing and landing face down on the grass. He did his best impression of the Pope and literally kissed the ground. They both lay there for the better part of an hour.

Connie spoke first. "You know, I had hoped that after the boat trip and seeing all those beautiful fish we'd go back to the room, shower, dress up nice, and go to a good restaurant. And then maybe a moonlight stroll on the beach, holding hands, and let nature take its course. I've always dreamt of making love on the beach. But now, if you come near me, I'm going to kill you."

They went back to the room and had toothpaste and mouthwash for dinner. Romance would have to wait – at least until the room stopped spinning.

Connie groaned and murmured to herself, "We should have gone to Toronto."

14. Romance on the Beach: Part II
From the Sublime to the Ridiculous

Library

"Will that be all, sir?" the ever-helpful librarian asked Blake.

"Yes, just the one CD."

"You know, we have other 'Soundscape' CDs here if you're interested. We have a crackling fire, a thunderstorm, and birds in the forest. And you can keep them for two weeks."

"No thanks, just the one CD will be fine."

"OK, sir. Have a nice day."

Liquor Store

"Well, honey, did you find everything you need?" the heavy-set, middle-aged cashier asked in a raspy voice with a cigarette dangling out of her mouth.

"Yes, I did. Thank you," Blake replied, trying not to wince as the acrid cigarette smoke stung his eyes.

"OK, one bottle of Captain Morgan rum and Pina Colada mix. Looks like a party to me!"

"I sure hope so," Blake smiled and replied as he walked out of the liquor store with his purchases.

The Neighbor

BLAKE WALKED UP the stairs of the red-brick, Georgian-style home and rang the bell. After a few moments, the door opened and Chuck Malatesta, his police officer buddy, smiled at Blake and asked, "What's up?"

Blake grinned and said, "Everything that should be. Listen, I was wondering if you could do me a favor."

"Sure, Blake. As long as it doesn't involve fixing your tickets."

"No, no. I gave up speeding for Lent. Anyway, I noticed you had some tiny, white, blinking lights on your bushes out front for Christmas decorations. I was wondering if I could borrow a string or two of those for a couple of days."

"The Italian lights?"

"Yeah, I guess that's what they're called."

"Do you know why they're called Italian lights?"

Blake shook his head and said, "No."

"Because they're not too bright!" Chuck laughed at his own joke and Blake groaned.

"Brave move on your part! A guy by the name of Malatesta telling anti-Italian jokes. You could get in trouble with the Mothers and Fathers Italian Association. You know, the Mafia."

It was now Chuck's turn to groan. He turned and said, "I've got them in the garage. But you just want one or two strings? I've got more. I've got colored ones too."

"No, just white – no colored ones. And one or two strings will be enough."

Chuck looked at Blake quizzically and asked, "Why do you want the lights?"

"I'd rather not say at this time," Blake replied. "But it's nothing illegal."

Chuck laughed, "Would you like a drink or something while you're waiting?"

"No, thanks. I'm kind of in a hurry."

"OK, suit yourself."

A few minutes later, Chuck returned with a small box of Christmas lights. Blake took the lights and turned to leave. Chuck asked him, "By the way, how was your trip to Florida?"

Blake paused and turned around for a moment and said, "Unfortunately, very windy and rainy. I'll tell you more later. Right now, I really have to run. Thanks for the lights."

The Auto Body Shop

"Hey, Mikey!" Blake called out to his friend, Mike McNamara. "How's it hanging?"

"Long and low. I had to tuck it into my sock."

"I know what you mean. I tripped on mine on the way over here."

Mike looked at Blake and grinned. "Why are you darkening my doorway? The usual car troubles?"

"No, I had a couple of questions about your shop. You guys do blasting to remove paint and rust, don't you? Do you use soda or sand or frozen carbon dioxide?"

"Mostly we use sand."

"Great. What type of sand is it?"

"Well, it's not like sandbox sand. This stuff is almost pure white and very fine. It also doesn't have any impurities in it, so we can shoot it out the nozzle with compressed air."

"I was wondering if I could buy some sand from you."

Mike scratched his head in confusion and said, "Uh...yeah. How much sand do you need? What do you want to do with it? The stuff isn't good for sandcastles. Doesn't stick together very well."

Blake grinned and replied, "Hey, I build all my sandcastles in the sky anyway. I only need about a coffee can full of sand."

"Yeah, but why do you need it?"

"It's a long story, Mikey. I'll tell you next week."

"OK. You got an empty coffee can?"

"Yeah, I have a clean one right in my car. I'll go get it. How much do I owe you?" he called back as he was leaving the shop to retrieve the can.

"Get the hell out of here. You don't owe me anything. I'll catch you the next time you need a lube job," Mike yelled after him.

When Blake returned a few minutes later Mike asked, "Hey, how did your trip to the Keys go?"

"Not so good," Blake replied, shaking his head. "It was very windy and very wet."

"I'm sorry to hear that. But hang in there, pal. Spring's a coming"

"Yeah, it is. The daffodils are starting to pop up all over. You should see Long Grove. They're all over the place. But I've still seen snowstorms in April. Sometimes I wonder why I live here."

Mike shook his head and said, "Me too, brother. Me too."

The House

CONNIE WAS DUE to arrive in about an hour and Blake was feeling giddy. He was scurrying about the house, gathering up every plant and placing them in the den. When he was done, the perimeter of the den was completely taken over by plants. In the center of the room, he had laid a queen-size beige sheet. He loaded his "Soundscape" disc into the CD player. The lights he had borrowed from his neighbor, Chuck, were strung along the upper branches of all the plants. He placed a chair just outside the den and looked around, checking to see if everything was perfect. Realizing he had forgotten the sand, he ran to his car, grabbed the coffee can, and sprinkled it all over the sheet. As he stood there admiring his work, he decided that comfort was important, so he ran upstairs, grabbed several pillows off his bed, and ran back down to place the pillows at the head of the sheet. He stood in the doorway and mentally checked off his list: *lights, sand, plants, and CD. Perfect*, he thought. *Absolutely perfect.*

He glanced at his watch, realizing that Connie would be there shortly. So, he closed the door to the den and raced to the kitchen. He read the directions on the Pina Colada mix, put everything in the blender, added the vanilla ice cream, and made a pitcher of frozen Pina Coladas. Retrieving two plastic tumblers from the cabinet, he filled them to the brim. He had neglected to buy pineapple, which bummed him out for a minute, but he did have some maraschino cherries and placed one in each tumbler. He thought the maraschino cherries were a nice touch because Connie had once bragged that she could tie the stem into a knot with her tongue. He was looking forward to seeing if her tongue was really that talented.

He ran back upstairs to the bathroom to check and make sure everything was ready there: two large beach towels, coconut-scented suntan lotion, and salt. Grinning, he ran back down the stairs. She would be here any second.

Just as he hit the bottom stair, the doorbell rang. *Oh shit*, he thought. *I forgot the blindfold. What to do, what to do? Oh hell, I could use one of those cloth napkins. Never use the damn things with a meal anyway.* He took a deep breath to calm himself and opened the door.

"Connie!" he exclaimed in a sing-song voice.

"Blake!" she exclaimed as she mimicked his tone. "You seem like you're in a chipper mood." They kissed briefly in the doorway.

"I am, I am. Come on in! I know I told you we would go to the movies tonight, but I've got a much better plan."

"So, what's your plan?"

"It's a surprise."

"A surprise, huh?"

"Yep, but first I've got a question. Do you trust me?"

"Trust you to do what? Not murder me in my sleep? Yeah, I guess so."

"But Connie, I trust you completely."

She smiled and said, "Sucker!"

"Connie, I'm curious. Have you ever been blindfolded?"

"Not since I was a kid when I beat the hell out of a pinata with a stick...Wait, what? You want to blindfold me?"

"Hey, let's have a drink first and then we'll talk." Blake smiled and led Connie into the living room. She sat down while he ran into the kitchen and came back with two Pina Coladas.

"Wow, Pina Coladas. This is festive," she said.

"I prefer to give you a Penis Colossus."

"Maybe later," she laughed.

Blake was anxious and excited. He felt he couldn't wait any longer. "Connie, he said, "I'm being serious now. Will you trust me for the next five or six minutes?"

"I suppose for five minutes I can trust you."

"All right, will you do what I tell you for the next few minutes?"

"I...guess...so..."

"Good. Now, take off all your clothes."

"You want me to take off all my clothes right now?"

"Yep."

"This had better not be too kinky," she replied as she began unbuttoning her blouse. "Don't you want me up in the bedroom?"

"No, actually I'm going to want you to sit in a chair right outside the den."

"You're really weird, Blake. You know that,

don't you?"

"Hey, I'm hurt. This is the first time I've ever been called weird," he paused then added in a low voice, "this evening."

When Connie was completely naked, Blake guided her to the chair just outside the den. "Now just sit here for a moment. I'll be right back." He ran off to the kitchen to get the cloth napkin. When he came back he said, "we were talking about blindfolds earlier and I'd like you to use this as a blindfold."

"You'd better not be planning on taking pictures or anything like that."

"Of course not," he responded. "Besides, I can't figure out where to get them developed." Blake placed the blindfold over her eyes and tied it gently. Her eyes were very sensitive and she wore contact lenses. He certainly didn't want to cause her any discomfort and ruin the moment. He knelt down next to the chair, kissed her passionately on the lips, and said "I'll be back in just a few moments." And with that, he abruptly left and bounded up the stairs, two at a time.

She called after him, "Hey, I'm getting chilly down here."

"I'll bring you something warm in a moment,"

he called down. Then he ran into the bathroom, stripped as fast as he could, turned on the shower, waited a moment until the water got tolerably warm, hopped in, got wet, and hopped out again. He grabbed the coconut-scented sunscreen and dabbed a little bit of it behind each ear. His fingertip was greasy with remnants, so he wiped it on his chest hair. He poured salt on his right hand, grabbed the two beach towels, and flew down the stairs.

He took Connie's right hand in his left hand and helped her stand up. He placed one beach towel over her shoulders, opened the door and tossed the other one into the den, and said, "Stand right here for a second." He ran into the den and started the CD that he had gotten from the library. Instantly the room was filled with the sound of waves crashing on the shore. He stepped out, took her hand, and led her into the den. He pressed his body against hers and kissed her enthusiastically, his tongue probing her mouth, seeking to do battle with hers.

She pulled away and said, "You're all wet! And you smell like coconuts."

He removed her blindfold and she stood there with her mouth hanging open while he explained,

"Well, you said you wanted to make love on the beach and Florida didn't work out for us. So, I thought I'd bring the beach into the house."

Connie looked around and exclaimed, "All the plants! And the lights!"

"They're meant to look like the stars," Blake explained.

"And the sound of the waves."

Blake stood there grinning. He led her into the den, onto the sheet where she felt the sand on her bare feet.

"My God, Blake! Sand?"

He embraced her again.

She said, "I get it now! You're wet from swimming in the ocean."

With that, Blake ran his fingers across her lips, and she tasted salt.

She asked, "Salt?"

"Well, it's an ocean beach, my dear," Blake said in a theatrically arrogant tone. "When one swims in the ocean, one comes out salty. Doesn't one?"

They kissed again. Blake's hands drifted slowly from her waist to cup her ass. He loved her ass. As he fondled it gently, she moaned softly. Suddenly, the sound of the waves was enhanced by the loud laughing sound of a seagull. She did her best to stifle her giggles but pulled away abruptly and began to laugh coupled with sputtering and choking. Brett started laughing also.

"Oh, I'm so sorry and embarrassed. I didn't mean to laugh at your efforts. It's just that the seagull..." At which point she began to laugh again.

"Come on. Lie down," he said. They laid down on the sand-covered sheet: he on his right side, she on her left. They started kissing again, their hands starting to explore each other's bodies. The seagull cried out again. This time they both laughed hysterically. They tried kissing again, but all they could do was laugh.

Connie looked at him and said, "Blake. Nobody has ever gone to this much trouble to make one of my fantasies come true. It's simply sublime."

Once again, the seagulls cried and Blake laughed, "Unfortunately, it has drifted into the ridiculous."

They spent the rest of the evening drinking Pina Coladas and laughing. They finally retired to the bedroom to make love and found that the sand Mike had promised would not stick to itself stuck very well to sweaty bodies and had burrowed itself into many inconvenient locations.

15. Chatterbox

JILL PULLED HER Subaru Outback into the parking lot of the Tradewinds grocery store in Blue Hill, ME. She looked in her purse to find her face mask. Instead, she found two and puzzled over which one to wear. There was a plain blue one and a green camo mask. Since she was wearing a green sweatshirt, she decided the camo one would match better. She laughed at herself. *It's hard to be stylish in the time of COVID. I wonder if bright orange masks will come in vogue during deer hunting season just like the bright orange hats do.* She put on her sunglasses because the sun would be directly in her eyes as she headed toward the store and because she knew that COVID could be transmitted directly to your eyes as well as your lungs. She gathered up her purse and her white canvas reusable Hannaford bags.

Stepping out of the car, she was excited to see an old friend who had been missing from her life for the past year or so. She raced up to her friend who was pushing a cart towards her car. Jill halted right in front of her friend's cart, blocking her progress. It wasn't six feet, but Jill felt it was distant enough. And besides, they both had on masks and sunglasses.

"How are you?" Jill questioned in an overly loud voice.

Her friend responded, "Uh, fine…"

Jill interrupted, "It's so good to see you. I've been meaning to call you." She looked over her friend, Sue, who was backlit by the late afternoon sun. Apparently, Sue had put on a little weight and her hair was a little longer, but that wasn't uncommon in the age of COVID.

"Listen, I've got so much to tell you," Jill began. "Do you have a minute?"

"Um, uh…"

"So, let me tell you. I finally got divorced. I know, I know. It's been coming for years. But Larry was such a worthless bastard. He'd come home from work, wolf down his dinner, go down in the basement, turn on the TV and drink beer. I counted one night – 17 beers. All he would do was fall asleep watching TV, burp, and fart. And our love life was terrible. He was always horny, but too drunk to perform. And the few times he was sober, he was so fast I never could enjoy it. But at least he was done quickly so I could get on with the laundry. I mean, I have needs too!

"So, anyway, I threw the bum out. And of course, the big baby moved back with his mommy. Now she can cook his meals and do his laundry. I tell you, I'm so glad to be rid of that worthless piece of shit.

"By the way, I'm feeling a lot better. As you know, for years I've been suffering from irritable bowel syndrome. Did you know there are two types of IBS? C and D. I don't know which would be worse, constipation or diarrhea, but I had diarrhea. For a long time, it was hard to go out. I was so afraid I would shit my pants or have to run to the bathroom. I probably shouldn't be talking about this, but you're an old friend and you knew about it, so what the heck. Anyway, I was watching TV and a commercial came up for Linzess. So, I actually followed the advice of the commercial and asked my doctor about it. She said that Linzess is more for constipation. But she offered me a different med. I forgot the name of it, but it plugged the leak. Now I shit like normal people. By the way, isn't it amazing what they have on commercials nowadays? They're talking about stuff they never would have when I was a kid. I mean, a woman having a period was never mentioned. Now they're dumping blue liquid all over maxi-pads to show how well they absorb. It's kind of gross, even if it is informative. And mentioning diarrhea? My God, that was never possible. They couldn't even show a toilet on TV. And forget talking about a gall bladder. The censors were afraid people would mistake it for the other bladder and think of pee. And how many ads are there for boner pills? I mean, do you remember that quarterback throwing the football through the tire? Talk about Freudian. So, I got my new prescription filled right over there at Rite-Aid." She pointed to the drug store next to Tradewinds. "And I'll tell you, it's been a miracle. And like I said, my symptoms have cleared up immensely. That's why I can now go to the grocery store and talk to you as easily as I can.

"So, between the divorce and the new meds, I got rid of two shits. Larry and the diarrhea."

Sue held up her finger and said, "Ah, I…"

"So, anyway, as I said earlier, a girl has needs, doesn't she? I mean, I know I'm getting older, but I'm not dead yet. I don't want my "twinkie" to grow cobwebs. So, I tried some online dating. A

CAPTAIN BILLY C.

couple of years ago, I couldn't do that here. I know I was married then, but once I got divorced, I thought I'd give online dating a try. We didn't have high-speed internet where I live in Surry until a couple of years ago and Larry, that cheap bastard, refused to pay for it. As soon as he was gone, I had it installed. I had to do something. Cell phone service is so terrible here. I hear they have better cell phone service in Calcutta than we do here. I mean, I couldn't set up a wi-fi hot spot. I could only have conversations in the kitchen. If I went into the living room with my cell phone the signal would drop.

"So now that I have high-speed internet, I was able to use my laptop and set up an online profile. I met this guy named Jack. We've been corresponding for a couple of months now and then we chatted on the phone a bit. From there, we advanced to meeting on Zoom. Isn't Zoom wonderful? I mean, I never heard of Zoom. Did anyone know what Zoom was before March? Now everyone's using it. I wish I had bought stock in that company. Anyway, I think he's kind of cute. And he has all his hair, not like the fat cue ball that I was married to. I mean, he had more hair on his ass than he did on his head. And as a bonus, Jack's got a good job. He's some sort of engineer. Not the train kind, but something to do with construction. I know he told me, but I kind of forgot. It either has to do with designing all the plumbing for the building or the electrical circuits for the building. I can't remember which. Anyway, we're actually going to get together this weekend. He's kind of quiet, but he seems to be a good listener, just like you."

"I..."

"Isn't it funny? His name is Jack and my name is Jill. If this works out, we'll be Jack and Jill. Isn't that so perfect? So, Jack is going to come up from Manchester, you know, in New Hampshire. It's a four-hour drive, so I invited him to spend the night in the guest room. But you know how that goes. To be on the safe side, we're both planning on getting tested for COVID just before he comes. And as long as we're both getting tested for that, we're also getting tested for STDs. You can't be too careful nowadays. After all, chlamydia is not a flower, you know! Yeah, I know I'm moving kind of fast on this, but it's really hard to find love in these times. Hell, it's hard just to maintain friendships. Look at us, we haven't talked in so long.

"I do have a question, however. I know it's the style now to shave your "hoo-hah." I've never done that before. Do you think I ought to? You know, just in case. I've never been a slave to fashion, but this seems kind of important and I don't want to appear "out of step" with what's going on. I mean, how do you even do that? I suppose I can use a razor, but the thought of making a slip terrifies me. And do I let it grow out or do I have to shave it forever? I mean, won't it itch when it starts growing out? And good grief, am I going to wind up with 5 o'clock stubble? How smooth do I have to make it? And where do I stop? Do I need a full Brazilian?

"And why is it called a Brazilian? Maybe it's got to do with those skimpy, thong bathing suits they wear down there. To me, it's more like butt-floss than a bathing suit. I just don't have the courage or the ass to wear something like that," she said, wiggling her rear end for emphasis. "Getting back to the Brazilian, I thought of using hot wax and duct tape, but c'mon! Ouch! I just can't picture myself with a melting candle and duct tape. By the way, is it duck or duct tape? I've seen it both ways. You'd think they would make up their minds.

"Listen, it's been so good talking to you. We really need to Zoom. I'm not sure I have your e-mail address. Let me get a paper and pencil so I can write it down." At this point, Jill opened her purse, fumbled with her shopping bags, and searched for a pen and paper.

Her friend held up her hand and said, "Stop. I just have two questions. Who are you? And who do you think I am?"

"I'm Jill, Jill Sargent. Aren't you Sue Thibodeau?"

"No. No, I am not."

"Well, who are you then?"

"I'm Sister Catherine Leo, up from St. Cecilia Parish in Boston."

Jill's face turned bright red. "I'm so sorry. You look just like my friend, Sue. You're a little heavier, though. Oh, shit…it's not like you're fat or anything. Oh, hell…I swore. I'm so sorry for all of this. I'm just going to go now and stick my head in the freezer."

As Jill ran into the store, Sister Catherine said to her back, "Uh, thanks for sharing…?"

16. Burning Desire

"I'M NOT KIDDING! I want you all to lather up with as much sunscreen as you can put on your lily-white bodies." Shari was lecturing her two sons and her husband with her hands on her hips.

"I know. I know, Mom," Gary, Jr. said while rolling his eyes at his mother. "But Dad and I are wearing shirts."

"I don't care. We're not that far from the equator and you can get a sunburn right through that t-shirt of yours. And Gary, dear," she said to her husband, "make sure you put some sunscreen on the top of your head. And wear a hat! You don't have as much hair as you used to, you know."

Donny, her youngest son, chimed in, "Yeah, Dad. You don't want to blind people with that chrome dome in the sun. You might cause a traffic accident just from the glare."

"Hey, if I want your opinion, Donny, I'll beat it out of you," Gary said, making a fist. Everybody laughed.

Shari was a schoolteacher who was used to dealing with teenaged boys. But most of all, she was a mom. And so, she perseverated as only a mom can do. "Listen, if you guys get burned, it's going to ruin the rest of the cruise. So, I want you to be careful. Furthermore, skin cancer runs in our family. So, the burn you get today may lead to a case of cancer in your future. I just want you to be careful."

The three males looked at her and sing-songed their response, "Yes, Mom, we'll be careful."

"I mean it! If you get burned, you'll get no sympathy from me."

The four of them continued to get ready in the cruise ship's tiny cabin, constantly bumping into each other. The two boys both wanted to use the bathroom at the same time. Gary, Jr. looked at Donny and said, "After you," with a graceful bow at the waist.

Donny replied, "No, no, I couldn't, sir. After you..." as he bowed.

"No, sir, I insist."

"Will you two clowns quit screwing around. The tender leaves in fifteen minutes and it's a long way down to deck five." Shari looked at her husband. "What excursion are you doing again?"

"Junior and I are doing the "Highlights of Grand Cayman" tour. We get on a bus that takes us right into George Town where we can walk around and shop for a bit. Since the drinking age is 18 here, I might even take Junior for a beer. Then the neat part of the tour is going to the turtle rescue facility where they have dozens and dozens of sea turtles that they are trying to rehab and set free.

Gary, Jr. interrupted his father and said, "I wonder how they teach them to use crutches!"

Shari glared at her son and said, "Junior!"

Gary, Sr., ignoring his wife and son, continued, "And you're going snorkeling with Donny, right?"

"Yeah, there's a snorkel shop a short walk from the pier where the tender docks. We go snorkeling right from there to see some sort of shipwreck. I think Donny will enjoy it."

The orange and white lifeboat that served as a tender provided a relatively smooth ride to the dock, by Grand Cayman standards. The waves splashed on the starboard side, being pushed by a strong breeze from the south. They were told that there are times when the winds are so strong, it's impossible for the tender to make it to shore safely. But this trip was uneventful. Once they were securely tied to the dock, Gary kissed his wife and he and Junior headed off to their bus while Shari looked for the snorkel shop. Spotting it a short distance away, Shari led Donny at a brisk pace toward the shack that would be their home base.

Behind the counter stood a tall, thin, blue-eyed, blonde man with dreadlocks who looked like he could be on a poster for a Beach Boys concert. Perhaps the best words to describe him were "overly tanned" and "scruffy chic."

"So, you guys are here to see our wreck?"

Donny replied, "I guess so."

"Great, dude. What size fins do you take?"

"I don't know. I wear a size 10 shoe."

"Size 7 fin should be about right, man. Let me look at your face...yeah, I've got a mask that will be perfect for you."

Shari said, "I wear a woman's 6."

"Gotcha," he said as he handed her some fins, then stared at her a moment and handed her a mask. "Can I have your names so I can check them off my list of cruise passengers?"

"Shari and Donny Garippo."

People were beginning to line up behind

CAPTAIN BILLY C.

them. The "surfer dude" began talking in a rather loud voice so other people in line could hear as well. "The wreck lies about one-minute swim straight out that way," he said, pointing vaguely to the water. "You can't miss her. She was a four-masted, steel-hulled schooner named the *Cali*. She was a large ship, 220 feet long. But in 1944, she was torn up pretty badly by a gnarly storm and sank right where she is now. The water's only about 30 feet deep there. With her masts sticking up out of the water, everyone was afraid a drunk fisherman would run into her. The governor decided the best thing to do was to blow her up, so the pieces scattered all over the bottom." The "big beach blondie" stopped, reached into a cooler, and pulled out a bottle of "Caybrew." After taking a long swig, he put down his beer and wiped the sweat from his forehead.

A heavyset man with a beet-red face in the back of the crowd asked, "Are there a lot of fish at the wreck?"

"Are there fish down there? Man, it's party central for all the beautiful fish. If you're a fish, it's the place to be!" After another pull of his beer, "Surfer Joe" grabbed a stack of plastic baskets from under the counter and said, "Anyone who wants to leave their shoes or any personal belongings, just put them in a basket and leave it on the counter. We'll keep them here for you. And chill! Nobody's going to steal your flip-flops!"

While Shari absolutely loved the water and felt entirely safe snorkeling, her 14-year-old son, Donny, wasn't quite so sure. While a decent swimmer, he had never snorkeled in the ocean before and was "concerned." He was concerned that he might be a tasty tidbit for a shark, barracuda, or even a moray eel. He had once heard a story of a moray eel chomping down on a snorkeler's hand and holding him under until the poor unfortunate soul drowned. Not wanting to appear nervous, Donny nonchalantly asked the beach-bum poster child, "Just curious, are there any dangerous predators by the wreck?"

"Not that you know of." The "salty dawg" immediately turned to wait on the next customer, stopping Donny from making any further inquiries.

After putting on their fins, the mother and son duo walked backward down the tiny beach and into the water. Their backward march kept their fins from digging into the sand in front of them, which could cause them to do a less than graceful face plant.

Sensing her son's angst, Shari said, "Donny, stick close to me. You'll be fine."

Within a minute, they realized that the "snorkel dude" hadn't lied. As they peered beneath them, dozens of fish appeared. The water was crystal clear, and they could easily see large pieces of the ship scattered about. Still concerned about sharks and barracuda, Donny peered left to right constantly, keeping an eye out for one of the nasty predators who might view his swimming trunks as a taco shell. French angelfish, parrotfish, blue and yellow tangs, and pufferfish all swam by in the first minute. Slowly, Donny began to relax. They swam further out to see more of the wreck and realized that the natural rocks in the area also held many wonders. Violet-colored fan coral swayed with the current. A warm-water spiny lobster scurried under some rocks. It was magical. Donny forced his body into a vertical position and started to tread water. He pushed his mask up to his forehead and his mom did the same.

"Mom, this is beautiful! I can't believe all the fish!"

"I told you that you would like it. Now put

your mask on, relax, and enjoy this. It's better than *YouTube*."

To save energy, the pair mostly floated on top of the water watching the seascape change from the wreck to beautiful rock formations. The warm water was almost body temperature and so they drifted…slowly…and peacefully…up and down…breathing rhythmically through their snorkel…in and out…in and out…losing all track of time and, unfortunately,…location.

Exactly how much time had elapsed is hard to determine. Thirty minutes? An hour? Two? They couldn't be sure how long they were floating. What brought them to their senses was the high-frequency whine of a propeller, getting louder and louder. They jerked upright just in time to see a large red and white boat turning sharply to avoid running over them. The driver of the boat yelled something unintelligible about the channel while shaking his fist. And while neither one could determine exactly what was said, they certainly could understand the message. They had drifted out of the dive site and way too far out to sea. When they turned around, they could see their cruise ship, but not the snorkel shack where they started their venture.

"Oh, my," Shari exclaimed as she pulled up her mask. "I think we're in the boating channel. We'd better start heading towards shore."

"Mom, there's no beach! All I see is a bunch of rocks."

"Well let's swim back to the beach and we'll be fine," Shari said, as they began their return voyage.

It didn't last more than a minute or two. Vertical once again, Shari said, "I think we're further away than we were when we started." Perhaps it was the ocean current or the southern wind that they encountered in the tender, but they were definitely heading north at a fairly good clip. All of Donny's concerns came back doubled.

Shari said, "Look, we're not going to drown. We'll get a little bit closer to shore and look for a place where we can climb out. You lead, I'll be right behind you."

Having the job of navigator relaxed Donny. Conserving his energy, he swam slowly and steadily, gradually getting closer to the shore. His mom called encouragement from behind. It took a while, but he finally managed to get them to a small sandy spot that was only a few yards wide.

From the little beach, they could see the pilings that held up a salty-looking, waterfront restaurant. The sign above the entrance said, "Da Fish Shack. Any Fresher and You'd Have to Slap Us!" An "Open for Dinner Only" sign, told them they wouldn't find help here. Nevertheless, a speaker hummed from the roof, broadcasting Jimmy Buffett tunes, "Yes, I am a pirate, 200 years too late. The cannons don't thunder, there's nothing to plunder, I'm an over-forty victim of fate. Arriving too late, arriving too late."

Shari looked at Donny and said, "Oooh! I love that song."

"Mom, focus! How are we going to get back? We can't swim. The current's too strong. And the rocks would tear our legs into bloody stumps."

"Honey, relax. We'll just take off our fins, climb up to the parking lot, turn right at the street, and walk back to the snorkel shop. Easy, peasy!"

They climbed up the small bluff wearing their dive masks on their heads and carrying their fins. They got up next to the parking lot, walked along a grassy edge to the sidewalk, turned right to head south, and screamed. The concrete that served as a sidewalk for North Church St. wasn't just hot. It was damned hot.

CAPTAIN BILLY C.

"Mom, we can't do this! Can't we just call a cab?"

"Two problems, Donny. Do you have your cell phone handy? Oh, it's probably next to your wallet with all your money in it to pay for the cab. Or perhaps we can use a phone booth. But first, we'd have to panhandle for change. And then we'd have to find, probably, the only telephone booth on Grand Cayman. I think we're stuck walking."

"But Mom, my feet were burning up the minute I stepped on the sidewalk. We can't swim back. We can't walk on the beach cause there's no beach. How are we going to get back?"

"Well, maybe if we jog it won't be so bad."

They began to jog. This lasted about twenty seconds until they found a small grassy spot and crowded onto it. "Ow, ow, ow," Donny whined.

"Well, that worked for a few feet," Shari said. "But I'm afraid if we did that for too long our feet would burst into flames. I heard there was a town called Hell on this island. I think we found it."

Donny laughed and said, "If this was the town called Hell, we could say our 'soles' were burning in Hell!"

"Ah, the joy of homonyms. You are your father's child, Donny."

"I suppose we could put on our swim fins," Donny said.

"It might come to that, but I'm afraid it would be too easy for us to get hurt. The sidewalk is not entirely even, so if we walk backward, one of us is going to trip and split their head open." Shari paused, smiled, and then said, "I've got it, Donny! You could carry me piggy-back. Then only one of us would end up with burned feet."

"That's not funny, Mom!"

"Lighten up, Donny. And it IS funny!"

"Wait a minute," Donny said. "What if we take one swim fin and throw it in front of us, run to that fin and stand on it and throw the other fin forward. Then we can step off the first fin, pick it up and run to the second fin and stand on it and keep going like that. Throw, run, stand, and repeat."

And that is what they did. Fortunately, there were no other pedestrians on this scorching day to observe mother and son leapfrogging the several blocks back to the snorkel shack. When they finally reached their starting point, the "surfer dude" had been replaced by a nearly identical, female counterpart. Shari and Donny turned in their masks while standing on their swim fins. When the "dudette" asked for their fins, they adamantly refused until she gave them their shoes back. Once fully shod, they realized their feet still burned as they climbed onto the tender to head back to their ship. Tender was the boat, and tender were their feet.

When Gary Sr. and Jr. returned to their cabin, they found Shari and Donny sitting on chairs with their feet wrapped in dripping wet towels loaded with chunks of rapidly melting ice.

"What the hell happened to you guys?" Gary, Sr. asked.

Shari and Donny alternated while telling the story of the "great flipper excursion."

"So, you two had to 'hot foot' it back here?" Gary, Jr. asked.

Shari groaned and Donny chuckled.

Gary, Sr. took off his hat and rhetorically asked, "Don't you think it's ironic? You worry about me burning the top of my head and you end up burning the bottom of your feet?"

Shari grimaced and replied, "Alright already! Give me a break. I'm in pain here. I deserve some sympathy."

"I seem to recall someone saying just a few

hours ago 'no sympathy' if we got burned." Gary, Jr. grinned, scratched his head, and continued, "You're telling us that after all your lectures on getting burned, you two Rhodes Scholars wound up burning the bottoms of your feet?"

"Hey, don't blame me! It was Mom's fault." Donny responded.

"You know, Mom," Gary went on, doing his best to imitate his mother's voice, "the burn you got today may lead to a case of 'toe-lio' in your future."

Shari looked at him and exclaimed, "Toe-lio! You moron. If I could stand up right now, I'd rip off your leg and beat you with the bloody end of it." But instead, she reached into the towel wrapped around her foot, pulled out a handful of crushed ice, and threw it at him. The three males simply grinned, utterly pleased with themselves.

17. Command Performance: Part I
The Poor Player

"So, are you going to do it or not?"

"I'm not sure. I haven't been in a play since I was in fifth grade."

"Oh, really? Who did you play?" Rob asked, feigning interest.

"An evil spider who's trying to eat Hansel and Gretel in *Babes in Toyland*."

"Typecast again, Billy?"

"Hey, it was a major part with absolutely no lines. My mom had to make my costume. She was a great cook, but a lousy seamstress. Even then, one night I forgot the string I was supposed to use to make the web, so I had to fake it."

Rob studied his friend intently. Billy was a heavyset man with a full beard and an infectious smile that he could turn off in an instant. Which is why Rob wanted him for the part. Billy, being a nice Italian man, could give the "evil eye" to anyone who annoyed him. He was like a character in an Italian gangster movie. Smiling and jovial one moment and glaring at you the next.

Rob continued, "Look, I've seen you perform at Second City. And I've seen you do professional presentations to hundreds of people at national Student Assistance Program conventions. For Christ's sake, you had your own television show on basic cable. What's so hard about being in a play?"

"It was a local access channel and was primarily informational. Anyone could do that. As for being in a play, it's very simple. I can't memorize lines."

"What do you mean you can't memorize lines? I've seen you on stage."

"Yeah, but that's different. Improv is all about creativity and spontaneity. There are only a few rules. Never say 'no' in a scene. It kills the action. Always say 'yes, and…'"

"Yes, and…?" Rob asked.

"In improv, if someone says something, like 'Look, over there. A water buffalo.' You don't say, 'There's no water buffalo over there.' That would kill the scene. What you do say, with an implied 'yes,' is 'And he's looking this way!' Yes, and… The other improv rule involves energy. Pump more energy into the scene. With acting, you want realism. With improv, you want more energy. The only other rule with improv is spontaneity and creativity. If you think of something go with it! That last one got me into trouble several times."

"Trouble? What kind of trouble?"

"You remember our special ed department staff meetings on Friday mornings? Well, Thursday night was my improv class. After class, we'd go to Kingston Mines, the blues bar right across from Victory Gardens Theater. So, I'd spend all Thursday night being spontaneous and creative and 'going with it,' followed by drinking heavily while listening to a blues band. The next morning, I was still wound up from Thursday night's class. I'd go to the 9 o'clock staff meeting, and I'd start doing schtick. You know you've gone too far when a meeting goes dead silent and all of the psychologists and social workers stare at you, some of them with their mouths hanging open."

Rob laughed. "I remember some of those meetings. You were hysterical."

"The boss sure didn't think so."

Rob continued his probing. "But what about all those SAP presentations about drugs and gangs? There were literally hundreds of educators in the audience at times."

"Again, that's different. I chose what I wanted to say, and I always had notes in front of me. I'd never write out the whole speech because reading a speech is boring. I always enjoyed talking in front of a large group. But those were my words, not somebody else's. With a play, an actor is merely a puppet on a string. He is told what to say, where to stand, how to move his hands, what his posture should be, all the way down to his facial expression. I could do most of that. The hard part for me, for some odd reason, is memorizing lines. I remember my freshman year in high school. Every time I screwed up in English class, the teacher had me write out Robert Service's poem, *The Cremation of Sam McGee*."

"That poem is funny!"

"I must have written out that poem fifty times because I was such a goof-off. I really wanted to memorize it because I thought it was a cool poem. 'The artic nights have seen queer sights, but the queerest they ever did see, was the night on the marge of Lake Lebarge I cremated Sam McGee.' And that's as far as I can go! You'd think I'd be able to memorize it, but I just can't."

CAPTAIN BILLY C.

"Well, in that case, this part is perfect," Rob said. "Your character has only about twelve lines of dialogue in the entire play. But everybody knows the part. Besides, this is only community theater. It's not Broadway. I'm already signed up to play Doc, Tony's boss at the drugstore. They've already got most of the high school kids cast for the rest of the characters."

"But Rob, this is a musical! I can't even hum on key."

"You don't sing at all."

"So, you really think I can play Officer Krupke?"

"Look, Billy, you're a natural for it! You've got one of the meanest looks I've ever seen. Most of the time you just stand around looking gruff, glaring at the teenagers. I hate to say it, but you're made for this role! And besides, it'll be fun! We can hang out together."

"OK, OK. I guess I can do this."

"Absolutely, Billy. Absolutely! And look on the brighter side. Only twelve lines to learn, and they actually sing a song about you. Anybody who's ever seen *West Side Story* remembers Officer Krupke. The only other character in the play that has a song about them is Maria. And you two will never be mistaken for each other." Rob said with a laugh.

"Hey, I'm trying to get in touch with my feminine side," Billy replied, trying to look offended. "When do we open?"

"We open up on Friday the 6th and there are ten performances."

Billy replied, "I guess I'm going to be a star." But the look on his face said he sincerely doubted it.

Rehearsal

JULIE, EVEN THOUGH she sometimes had her doubts, believed in supporting her husband in whatever crazy endeavor he got into. This time, however, she actually liked the idea of Billy performing in a play. She had acted in many community theater plays from high school into her twenties. After only a few readings of a script, or hearing other actors perform, she could memorize not only her lines but the lines of her fellow actors.

"Billy, there are only twelve lines. It's less than a hundred total words. How can you keep screwing them up?" she asked with a justified amount of exasperation.

"I don't know. Krupke says things in a way I wouldn't. All right, this time for sure. I have gone through my lines at least a hundred times and this time I'm sure I've got it. Let's go through it one more time. The play's tomorrow. I have to get this down, pat."

Julie sighed and, without looking at the pages, fed him his cue. But, true to form, Billy immediately flubbed his lines, yet again.

Closing Night

JULIE WAITED FOR Officer Krupke in the lobby after the final performance. She was smiling broadly when Billy and Rob, still in costume, appeared. People were patting Billy and Rob on the back, congratulating them on their great performances. The two men walked up to her.

Rob looked at Billy and said, "I told you that you could do it."

"Yeah, you did. But I'm really glad it's over. You wouldn't believe how hard it was for me to memorize my lines."

At this point, Julie lost it. "Memorize your lines? I've been to every one of the performances.

And you never once said your lines the way they were written. Nor were they ever the same two nights in a row. You improvised every performance."

"They were really different?"

"Yes, Billy, yes. They were really different. Every time! How could you not know this?"

At that moment, a thirty-something blonde woman put her hand on Billy's shoulder, looked him in the eye, and said, "You were so real. Your look scared me, even in the audience. Are you really a cop?"

Billy laughed and said, "No. But, I believe in method acting. I've studied Stanislavsky."

Julie and Rob just looked at each other. After the woman left, Rob and Julie laughed and Julie said, "You're such a bullshitter. Stanislavsky, my ass. You can't even spell Stanislavsky!" Julie threw up her hands in exasperation, "Nobody in the audience ever realized that your performance was completely off-script. Your fellow actors had to adapt their own lines to follow whatever you said."

Billy took off his police cap and scratched his head. "They never complained to me."

Julie replied, "Perhaps it was out of respect for

a man of your age."

Billy glared at her. She continued, completely unintimidated. "But more likely it was out of fear. You really did look like you could 'eat their livers with a nice Chianti'."

Billy thought for a while, as the crowd slowly drifted away. "You know, I really like performing on stage. Maybe I should try stand-up!"

18. Command Performance – Part II
Interview with a Comedian

THE APPLAUSE DIED down and people began to leave. Billy's friends gathered around him and congratulated him on a great routine. They slapped him on his back and invited him to get a drink across the street at TGI Friday's. He knew he could use one, so he readily agreed. Billy glanced at the stage where he stood only minutes earlier. He couldn't believe he had actually performed there. He was excited and exhausted at the same time. He was definitely looking forward to that beer. But, as he was preparing to leave, a thin, middle-aged man wearing glasses came up to him, introduced himself, and handed him his card. It read, "Jeff Watson, Reporter, Pioneer Press." Billy looked at him quizzically.

"Billy," the man said, "I'm a reporter and I was wondering if I could interview you for an article in the local paper."

"Why?" Billy questioned. Although Billy was

anxious to leave, he was puzzled and intrigued.

"Pioneer Press likes to cover local cultural events and your routine was very funny. I'd like to do a story about what it's like to go up on stage and perform for the first time."

"Ummm, OK. But not right now. I'm meeting a bunch of friends across the street for a much-needed drink. And they're buying, so I don't want to be late. Would tomorrow work for you?"

"I believe so. What time?" asked Jeff.

"How about 5 o'clock at On the Border? Do you like Mexican food?"

"Absolutely. 5 o'clock will be fine. We can talk over beer, chips, and salsa.

By the way, Billy, can I have your phone number in case something comes up?"

Billy rattled off his phone number and just when he was about to leave another audience member stopped him. It looked like it would be a while before he could get his much-needed drink.

Next Day

BILLY WALKED INTO On the Border and immediately saw Jeff sitting at a booth close to the entrance. He nodded to the overly eager hostess saying,

"I'm meeting someone," as he strode over to the booth and plopped down. Jeff was drinking what looked like a Coke with lime, or perhaps a "Cuba Libre." The waitress sashayed over. She was dressed like all the other waitresses at this restaurant. Tight black pants and a very loose-fitting white Mexican peasant blouse with a scooped neckline. She leaned over, providing excellent service with a peek. Billy ignored the view and ordered a Negro Modelo.

On the Border was a cavernous restaurant with high ceilings. The dining area was big enough to seat hundreds of people at the same time, but the dinner crowd had yet to arrive, so it was relatively quiet. A large Rube Goldberg-like machine behind glass walls at the back of the restaurant was humming along, churning out "homemade" tortillas. With all of its levers and wheels, it reminded Billy of a 1930s steam engine. The décor was exactly what you'd expect in a suburban Mexican restaurant. Gaudy sombreros, Mexican blankets, guitars, and other paraphernalia festooned the walls. In essence, the restaurant was garishly furnished with sale items from a Tijuana gift shop. The air smelled of a mixture of beer, fried onions from the sizzling fajitas being

CAPTAIN BILLY C.

served, and the tangy, vinegary smell of the mandatory salsa. The waitress stopped by their table and leaned over to provide Billy's beer and that "oh, so important" peek.

"Are you gentlemen ready to order?" she asked.

Jeff said, "I'll just have some guacamole and chips." Billy ordered white queso with chorizo and the waitress left to turn in their orders.

"Thanks for coming, Billy. By the way, I enjoyed your performance last night. Please tell me if I'm wrong, but this was really your first time doing stand-up comedy?"

"Yes and no," Billy replied. "I've done some comedic bits in front of my co-workers, but that was different because everybody knew me, and I knew all of them. So, the stress level is very different. This was the first time I performed in front of a large group of strangers. While I knew some of the people in the audience, I had never met 90% of them."

"Why did you choose to do this?"

"I didn't lose a bet if that's what you're wondering. I chose to do it because it's hard. And I wanted to see if I dared to stand up in front of a bunch of strangers and make them laugh. I've done some improv in the past, but improv involves a group of people that work together as a team. Stand up is purely a solo act. If improv isn't funny, you can always throw your teammates under the bus and blame them. If you're doing stand-up and no one laughs, there's only one person you can blame. I guess I wanted to find out number one if I had the guts and number two if I was funny enough that the audience would laugh at my jokes. My intention was just to do it once, to see if I could."

Billy sipped his beer and continued, "I work full time in the school system and I'm not looking to change careers this late in life. I think I'm pretty good as an amateur, but it would take way too long, and I would have to work way too hard to reach a professional level. I just can't see being out late, night after night doing open mics in smoke-filled bars. My wife is tolerant, but not THAT tolerant."

"This was part of a class at Zanies Comedy Club?"

"Yes, it was an eight-week course and our final exam was doing the stand-up routine in front of a live audience. In education, this is called 'authentic assessment.' Don't tell me how you would do it. Do it."

"Did the class have any rules or give you any advice?"

"There were several rules we all followed. If you notice, there were no dirty jokes. Mine was probably the dirtiest, and at worst it's PG. Our teacher, Toby Gladwell, laid it all out in the first class. Number one, keep it clean. Number two, absolutely no 'dick jokes,' which I thought was kind of redundant. Number three, no internet jokes. And number four, no stealing from other comedians. All the jokes had to be written by you."

Jeff was taking notes and he looked up and asked, "Is it hard to write a joke?"

"It was for me. It also seemed like it was pretty hard for the rest of the people in the class. It probably took me 40 hours to come up with a seven-minute routine. It was harder than writing an essay final on Greek and Roman history. Although the material had to be original, we were allowed to do substitutions on jokes."

"Substitutions?"

"In substitutions, the nature of the joke stays the same, but you change the details."

Jeff raised his right eyebrow. "Hmmm. I'm not

sure I follow you."

"OK, let me give you an example," Billy said. "If I give you an apple and cut it in half, what do you have?"

"Two pieces?"

"And if I cut those in half, what do you have?"

"Four quarters, or four pieces."

"What do you have if I cut it in half a thousand times?"

"I give up."

"Applesauce."

Jeff chuckled softly and said, "OK."

"Now the substitution. What do you get if I give you a large piece of wood?"

"A large piece of wood."

"What if I cut it in half?"

"I get two pieces of wood."

"And if I cut it in half a thousand times, what do you have?" asked Billy.

"OK, I'll bite. What do I have?"

"Toothpicks. You see," Billy continued, "it's the same joke. You just change the details."

"Interesting." Jeff continued scribbling his notes.

Whether or not Jeff found it interesting was impossible for Billy to tell. Although he smiled a lot, Billy couldn't tell if he was really pleased or just politely feigning interest. Billy decided he would hate to play poker with this guy. But he was on a roll now and he continued explaining the joke writing process.

"One of the old rules on writing jokes, dating probably back to vaudeville, is that 'P' and 'K' words are funnier than other words. That's why Don Rickles called people hockey pucks rather than baseballs. The other comedic guideline that helped me a lot was hyperbole. If you're going to describe something, make it bigger or smaller than it could realistically be. And that makes it funnier. The goal in comedy is to get a laugh. It is not to give a news report. My one joke about the June bug is a perfect example of that. When I originally wrote it, I described the June bug as being as big as a sparrow. But it is funnier when I describe the June bug as the size of a B-52."

"Yeah, I see what you mean," Jeff interjected.

"I guess one of the other rules about everybody's performance was to say nothing hurtful. I had a line that I self-censored. After I got hit by the June bug, I stated that it left a red welt right in the middle of my forehead. 'I could have opened up my own 7-11.' But I cut that line because it was too racist and could be deemed hurtful."

Jeff looked up from his notepad again and asked, "What was the scariest part?"

"Basically, waiting around. I was the last performer. So, I got to watch all my classmates before I could go up. It drove me nuts. And then I watched one of the women blow one of her jokes. It was a setup joke. She set something up early in the routine. Then she would circle back to it about two minutes later and deliver the punch line to the setup. I've seen her do that joke many times. But, when she was performing, she blew the setup, so the punch line wouldn't work. Instead of a big laugh, she got a big silence. That terrified me. I was afraid I would do the same thing.

Jeff said, "You didn't seem to mess up any of your lines."

"Yeah, well, I cheated."

"How do you cheat in comedy?"

"Some performers write a brief outline of their routine on their hand. And if they get lost in their routine, they can look down at their hand, figure out where they are, and continue with their routine with no one being the wiser. By the way, certain politicians do the same thing. It helps keep them on point."

CAPTAIN BILLY C.

Jeff objected. "I saw your hands. You had nothing written on them. So how did you cheat?"

Billy laughed. "I'm Italian. I have to use my hands when I talk. And my comedy required a lot of hand gestures, so I couldn't write on my hands. I had to use a cheat sheet. Most cheat sheets are really small, so the audience doesn't see them. I always have trouble remembering my lines. So, I made a giant cheat sheet out of poster board. And I had my wife sit right up in front of the stage with the poster board facing me, flat on the table. If I lost my place, I could just look down and see the outline of my routine."

Jeff incredulously stated, "I never saw it."

"That was the whole point."

At that moment, the waitress returned with their food. Billy ordered another Negro Modelo while Jeff seemed content with what he had. After the waitress left, Jeff ate a few chips with the guacamole, sipped his drink, and continued the interview.

"Did you have any comedic idols in mind when you did your routine?" Jeff asked while dipping his chips in the guacamole.

"Actually, I did. There are several types of comics, and I love them all. Steven Wright is hysterical, but he is so far out in left field that I couldn't hope to match his style. Jack E. Leonard and Don Rickles are great insult comics. They are like bullfighters. They improvise all their jokes and maneuver the audience around while continually jabbing with little spears of insults. This style of comedy was big during the 70s and 80s, but it seems to be dying out today in the 90s. And I'm just not that fast. Also, I would be too afraid of hurting someone's feelings. Next, there are joke tellers like Bob Hope, Rodney Dangerfield, and Henny Youngman. Those guys will do hundreds of jokes in an hour. I can't write that many. Then there are the storytellers. These are my heroes. Rita Rudner, Paula Poundstone, Carolyn Rhea, and Bob Newhart. These comedians take incidents out of their own lives and stretch them out with tremendous detail and deliver hilarious routines. I modeled myself after this latter group. I always viewed myself as a storyteller. The question I had was, were my stories funny enough to entertain strangers while on stage."

Jeff had managed to finish his meal while Billy continued with his soliloquy. Billy realized he had been talking too much and asked "Hey Jeff,

CAPTAIN BILLY C.

what twelve-step program is there for compulsive talkers.

Jeff furrowed his brows and shrugged his shoulders.

"On and on Anon! I guess I'm late for a meeting."

Billy began to eat feverishly before his queso could cool enough to form a superball-like mass. Jeff signaled for the waitress to bring his check and Billy received his second beer.

"Is it possible for me to get a copy of your routine?" Jeff asked. "I'd like to quote some of your jokes."

"I guess so."

"Can you e-mail it to me? The address is on the card I gave you last night. With a little luck, the story will appear in Sunday's paper, in the Arts and Entertainment section."

"Cool! I'll look forward to reading it," Billy said.

"One last question before I go, Billy. Were there any surprises?"

"The first surprise shouldn't have happened because I was warned ahead of time. When you're standing on the stage, the lights are so bright in your eyes you cannot see the audience in front of you. Just the first few tables. You can hear them, but you can't see them. This is bad because if they're not laughing loudly, you can't tell if they're enjoying the show and smiling amusedly or if they're loading a gun. It's hard to continue without the feedback.

"But the biggest surprise came after the performance. Remember I said I was only going to do this once and never again? After I talked to you, catastrophe struck. One of the guys from the audience came up to me, said he was the leader of a comedic troupe that did a lot of performances at corporate retreats. And then the son-of-a-bitch offered me a job!"

19. Command Performance – Part III
Itching to Be a Man

"GOOD EVENING EVERYBODY. Welcome to the *Zanies* of Vernon Hills, kind of the cultural mecca of the northwest suburbs. My name is Billy C and I'll be your entertainer for the next five minutes or so.

"What I wanted to talk about is an idea that's been kind of bouncing around in my head for the last couple of years – and that is that it's very hard to be a man in the 90s. In fact, it's really hard for me to feel like a man in the 90s. I mean, my dad fought the Germans in the Ardennes. My brother fought the Viet Cong at Chu Lai. Me, the only thing I ever fought was the Xerox machine when my damn tie got caught in the automatic document feeder," Billy said as he pulled his head down by yanking on his tie.

"Hey, it's hard to feel like a man. So, I did something to try and make myself feel more manly. I went out and bought myself a motorcycle. Yeah. Now, if you want to be a man, there's really only one kind of bike to buy – a Harley Davidson. I got me this beautiful Low Rider with the big 'ape hangers.' Everything on the bike was chrome. It was beautiful! The only problem with it, it really vibrated a lot. Which is probably why my girlfriend liked it a lot better than I did. She used to sit on the back of the bike kind of leaning forward hitting me in the back of the head yelling, 'Go faster. Go slower. Go faster. Go slower. Faster, faster, faster, faster'." Billy whacked himself on the back of the head repeatedly.

"Like to give me a migraine... But it ended kind of sadly though. She did leave me – for her own motorcycle. She said it had a bigger engine with a much thicker piston. I don't know. I think it was a Yamaha Viagra or something like that.

"Now if you buy a motorcycle, you have to maintain it and you have to clean it. You can't just take it through a car wash. I suppose you could, but you'd get very moist. So, what I did was I took this bike and I put it right on the corner in front of my house. And I'd wash the bike. And little kids would gather around, you know, because they were admiring the motorcycle. And

CAPTAIN BILLY C.

I'd use the Miyagi method to clean it." Billy made circular motions with his hands. "Wax on, wax off. Wax on, wax off.

"Now it was working! These kids were really getting into this. They really were. And it probably would have worked out alright for me, if I had only read the directions on the bottle of ArmorAll, which said 'Do not use on a motorcycle seat. It will make it slicker than snot.'

"I polished up the seat real nice, see, and I get on the bike. And remember, the little kids and the teeny boppers are all still gathered around. I gotta leave fast, I gotta move. I gotta show them how cool I really am. So, I got on that bike and I cranked the throttle and 'Wham.' The next thing I know my butt has left the motorcycle and I am flying through the air like the caped crusader." Billy leaned forward with his arms outstretched to the imaginary handlebars. "I'm barely hanging on, screaming at the top of my lungs, and the only thing I can do to save myself is to reach forward with my right hand, grab the front brake, and 'Whoom'." Billy jerked his hands up behind his ears. "Now, I'm paying an unintended conjugal visit to my gas tank. And, I'm wearing a big smile cause the handlebars are stuck in my teeth.

"I tried to pretend like I meant to do it, but even the little kids were going, 'Uh uh, no way dude. Nah. We ain't buying that.' So, I gave up trying to show off.

"I go off and ride alone, on Sunday mornings. You know, get up early before there's any traffic. And go out on these country roads like Gilmer Road, out here. A nice, winding road that runs through these farmer's fields. And if it's a real early morning, there's sometimes mist on the field. And it's just beautiful. And I'm all alone. And I start singing to myself the national anthem of motorcyclists. *Born to Be Wild*. See, and I didn't care. I was off-key, but it didn't matter. Because I was really in the moment and enjoying myself. And it gets to the part," Billy started singing, "Lookin' for adventure. Or whatever comes my way. WHAP!" Billy hit himself in the forehead.

"What came my way was a June bug the size of a B-52. This thing was so big, it blotted out the sun. There were little Japanese fairies next to the road chanting 'Moth-a-ra, Moth-a-ra.'

"So, I had to get myself a helmet. And again, if you're trying to be a man, you can't buy just any old wimpy white helmet. No, I got myself this Darth Vadar-looking sucker. I mean it was beautiful. It was all black, came down here," motioning to his chin, "had these great air vents on the bottom. And a black shield. So, you couldn't even see my eyes. And I looked scary. And I felt safe. I'd be riding, and I felt invulnerable 'cause I had my helmet on.

"Then I discovered the design flaw. It seems that, if you have to sneeze inside your motorcycle helmet, there is no way to cover your 'Achoo'." Billy splayed his hand in front of his face. "Now, I am looking at a psychedelic kaleidoscope of multi-colored mucus. And no matter which way I turn my head, it's still there.

"At this point, it starts to rain. Now, rain is OK on a bike, if you've got your helmet on and you're wearing a leather jacket or a rain jacket. I mean, you stay pretty dry because the water hits you and just rolls down the front of your body. And stops right about here." Billy moved his hands down his body to his groin. "Forming an ice-cold, vibrating little puddle right at your crotch.

"And that's not the worst part. The worst part is when the rain stops, and you get off your bike and you walk around town. And you've got this wet spot right about here. Little kids are pointing and laughing – they think it's an inside job. An old lady walks up to me and hands me a coupon for Depends.

"But you know, the next morning I woke up and I realized, I had achieved my goal. I finally felt like a real man. I had the worst case of jock itch that Gold Bond medicated powder had ever seen.

"Thank you very much, you've been great!"

20. Legend in His Own Mind

BY ANY STRETCH of the imagination, police Chief Derrick Heinrich was "squared away," except for the fact that everybody knew him, and everybody hated him. Criminals hated Chief Heinrich because he was rather hard-nosed and never gave anyone a break. His men hated him because he was an insufferable prick, and he never gave them a break either.

Chief Heinrich was a tall, handsome man with piercing blue eyes. His short-cropped black hair showed just a touch of gray at his sideburns. He was always clean-shaven. His uniform was neatly pressed and form-fitted to his physique. He always stood ramrod straight and never slouched. He was lean and exceptionally fit. His holster sheltered a nickel-plated Colt revolver. Although his gun set him off from the rest of the police force, who all had black guns, what truly made him unique were his boots. They rose rather high on his legs with his neatly pressed trousers tucked inside. His boots were so shiny you could easily see your face reflected on their surface. This led to the third group who hated him – the teenagers in town. They could spot his arrogance from miles away and they derisively called him "Officer Fruit Boots."

Chief Heinrich had spent several years in the Army Reserve, but he viewed himself more as a Marine drill instructor. His heroes included Jack Webb, in the movie *The D.I.*, and General Patton. Although he was not a Nazi by any stretch of the imagination, he did admire the intimidating black Gestapo uniforms and wished he could dress in the same way. He also admired the German penchant for cleanliness and orderliness.

The fact that Chief Heinrich was employed by a peaceful suburban town didn't stop him from constantly demanding perfection from his men. He was fond of inspecting them every chance he could. In the '70s there were very few female police officers and his command only had two. He didn't hate them. In fact, he was rather afraid of them because he didn't know how to relate to them. If pressed, he would probably say that they were OK, as long as they kept their mouths shut, did what they were told, and didn't bring up any "girly" issues. Mostly he ignored them, which was probably best for all parties concerned.

One Friday at 4 pm, he noticed an officer coming off his shift. The officer, a 25-year veteran of the department, had a small coffee stain on the front of his shirt. The chief blew a gasket. His face turned bright red and blood vessels stood out at the temples of his head.

"What is the meaning of this?" he interrogated the hapless victim in front of all the other officers who were changing shifts.

"Sorry, sir. I just spilled some coffee," Officer Jenkins explained as he looked down at where the shirt was stretched over his expanding waistline.

"Do you realize you represent this department to the entire public? Do you realize that this makes me look like a commander who cannot effectively discipline his officers? Where is your pride?!" The screaming and questions and accusations went on and on, culminating in derogatory comments about the man's girth before he abruptly dismissed the "properly" chastised officer.

Jenkins went down to the locker room, grumbling something about "If this was Vietnam, he would have been fragged years ago." The officers around him all sympathetically agreed.

The "incident" happened just a few days later. Chief Heinrich decided to inspect the locker room at about 3 pm between shift changes. He knew no one would be in the locker room until 4 pm when officers both got off and came on duty. Not surprisingly, he wore white gloves. The locker room was old and rather cramped. *It could **definitely** use a coat of paint*, he thought. But the town was broke and didn't have the budget to decorate a police locker room, particularly since it was never seen by the tax-paying public. He pressed his fingers into a bullet hole that adorned one of the lockers. Apparently, years before he became chief, one of the policemen dropped his gun and it fired a shot into the locker. No one was hurt, and no one ever claimed responsibility. And even though the incident took place before his time, he felt personally insulted by its mere presence.

The lockers were primarily divided into two banks about six feet apart facing several changing benches laid end to end between them. Another small set of lockers was placed at the far end of the room perpendicular to the benches. The lockers were about seven feet tall and were gun-

CAPTAIN BILLY C.

metal gray. Several were dented and others had small patches of rust on their corners. He could see a few small dust bunnies in the corners of the room on the dingy, brown linoleum. "This place is a pigsty," he muttered to himself.

Being the thorough man he was, he decided to step up on the first changing bench. He was looking at the tops of the lockers to find more dust bunnies and perhaps something that might not belong on top of "his" police lockers. He leaned over to the lockers on his right and ran his white-gloved hand over the top and found, horror of horrors, DUST! He side-stepped his way down the length of the lockers finding more and more dust, a moldy old deck of cards, mouse droppings – and he grew angrier and angrier. He decided to check the small group of lockers at the end of the benches as well. He did a full military pivot and marched purposefully to the last bench. He was determined to inspect everything and write a full report to the town manager about the disgusting filth he found in his department. He had just reached the far end of the bench and stood on its edge to peer over at the lockers facing him when suddenly there was a bright flash of light and he lost consciousness.

A short time later, when the officers arrived to change shifts, they found him lying unconscious with the changing bench uprooted from its stand and lying nearly on top of him. It seems that Chief Heinrich rediscovered the old Archimedes principle that led to the development of the lever and the teeter-totter. His weight on the extreme end of the bench, unfortunately, pulled out the floor fasteners at the opposite end. The bench whacked him in the back of the head which accounted for the bright flash, the loss of consciousness, and the concussion that he suffered.

A small crowd of police officers gathered around the prone chief of police. They muttered amongst themselves, wondering what to do.

One officer asked, "What happened?"

Another whispered, "Maybe it's a trap and he's just faking."

"I'll go call an ambulance."

"He's still alive. I can see him breathing."

Suddenly they all heard a shout, "I've got this!" Officer Jenkins decided the best thing to do was to revive him by retrieving a bucket of mop water from the nearby maintenance closet and gleefully throwing it on his face. As the chief sputtered to confused consciousness, his men snickered, quietly giggled, and choked as they tried to suppress outright belly laughs.

The story of "the incident" spread like wildfire. The officers talked about it to each other, then to the rest of the department, then to their friends in other departments, to their families, and the friends of their families. One of the officers even violated the sacred protocol of the "blue wall of silence" and blabbed to the press – anonymously of course. The newspaper article about "the incident" was titled *Police Chief Injured in Workplace Incident*. The story became so much a part of local folklore that it outlasted the chief's retirement and was shared in bars for decades to come. Chief Derrick Heinrich went from being a "legend in his own mind" to a "legend in his own time."

21. Saving a Life: Part I
Damsel in Distress

BEN WAS WALKING rapidly south on Rush St. when he guiltily stopped to look at a picture of a naked woman wearing only a g-string and pasties. He knew he wasn't supposed to be walking by the strip club, but it was late in the day and he figured nobody from the Catholic school would catch him. He stared at the image in the window for a moment and his eyes changed focus so he could see his face.

His acne wasn't too bad, he thought, just one stupid zit on his right cheek. He also noticed that his dark "James Dean-like" hair was starting to freeze as he had just come from the pool. He laughed to himself about this. He had learned that when your hair freezes after it has been combed just perfectly, it won't fall out of place for the rest of the evening. He had just turned fifteen and decided, as he looked at himself, that he was average. He wasn't too tall nor too short. He may

CAPTAIN BILLY C.

have been a little heavy, but as an Italian, he felt that was OK. There was nothing that made him stand out from the crowd, and that was just fine with him.

He knew he wasn't an athlete. His eye/hand coordination was mediocre at best, so he was out of luck when it came to many sports. The two things he could do were swim and float, so he spent a lot of time doing just that. In fact, that's why he smelled of chlorine. Fortunately, he liked the smell.

It was brutally cold, and the wind was howling past the Chicago Water Tower, so he picked up his pace. A few snow flurries streaked horizontally past his rapidly numbing ears. He turned west on Chicago Ave., passed the hot dog stand, and headed toward the State St. subway. He could hear the music from the jukebox playing the Top-40 hit from Chubby Checker – *The Twist*. He had a long way to go to get home. It was rush hour and he'd have to stand on the overcrowded subway. But at least it would be a warm, though smelly, ride.

He had stayed after school taking a Red Cross lifesaving class. He wanted desperately to be a lifeguard. Actually, that's not quite true. He did not necessarily want a job as a lifeguard. What he wanted was to save a beautiful girl from drowning. He wanted to be the hero and to feel her unending gratitude for saving her life. This wish was his secret, yet burning, desire. His compulsion. Little did he know his wish would be granted, but not in the way he thought.

Five years later

WONDER LAKE IS a six-mile-long man-made lake, formed by the damming of the Nippersink Creek. It lies approximately sixty-five miles northwest of Chicago – not too far from the Wisconsin border. Several of the beaches were creatively named Beach #1, Beach #2, and, surprisingly enough, Beach #3.

Ben and his long-term girlfriend, Mary Jane, along with his best friend, Chuck, and his new date, Carol, were sitting on a small cement and stone wall that divided the grass from the sand. Beach #2 was small. The sand was only ten feet long before it reached the water and only about one hundred feet wide. They were the only four people there.

Both Ben and Chuck were dressed in nondescript dark swim trunks. Whether they were black or blue was hard to determine unless they were in bright sunlight and you looked really carefully. Mary Jane wore a two-piece aqua-colored swimsuit which made her red hair stand out even more than usual. It was also a sharp contrast with her pale, white skin and freckles. While she was in excellent shape, the suit did little to flatter her figure. Although the bathing suit was a two-piece, it was as far from a bikini as you can imagine. The top was modest, and the bottom was high enough on her waist to hide her navel. She had little desire to attract male attention to herself. She lingered on the wall, not particularly anxious to go in the water because the truth of the matter was, she couldn't swim, and much preferred the safety of the shallow end of a swimming pool.

Chuck had only met Carol two days before and they were in that awkward stage of the relationship having stilted conversations, trying to figure out who each other was. In contrast to Mary Jane, Carol's bathing suit was a one-piece. But what a one-piece it was! It was cut high up on her hips and had an open space between the right half and left half of the suit covering her breasts. A string, similar to a shoelace, laced back and forth across her chest – much like a gym shoe's lace crossing over the tongue of the shoe. Only the gaps were much further apart, both vertically and horizontally. The suit was a bright red that complimented her blonde hair. Rather than showing simple cleavage, the entire area between her breasts was visible in a peek-a-boo fashion from the very top of her suit all the way down below her belly button.

Carol had not decided whether she liked Chuck enough to go on a second date with him at that point. As their conversation soared and lagged, they both chain-smoked cigarette after cigarette. Chuck couldn't keep his eyes off her bathing suit. Or, more accurately, the space between it. When Ben glanced over for a peek himself, Mary Jane would either elbow him or shoot him a dirty look.

Finally, after about the fifth cigarette, Chuck and Carol decided they would swim out to the raft, which was located only fifty feet from the shore. Neither Chuck nor Carol were strong swimmers. They huffed and puffed their way like tugboats, creating more splash than momentum as they struggled to get to the raft. They then decided to race back to the shore, which, in retrospect was a completely stupid idea.

Chuck was winning the race but coughing and wheezing at an alarming rate. He barely made it to shallow enough water to stand up when Carol started screaming. Ben and Mary Jane both jumped to their feet. Ben looked at Mary Jane and said, "she's probably just screwing around, waiting for Chuck to rescue her. Pathetic!"

Chuck looked at Carol struggling in the deeper water and just stood there. There was no way he could swim back out to her and return to shore. He had barely made it himself. Ben said, "Aww, hell," and ran into the water.

He was sure Carol was only faking her distress, so he swam directly to her. She immediately grabbed his head and pushed him under. His face was now buried between her breasts, underwater. Several thoughts raced through his head at once. He was embarrassed by the fact that his nose was actually between her boobs and that's exactly where he wanted to be and didn't want to be at the exact same moment. His second, and more important thought, was, *Hey, she really is drowning*. He came to this conclusion because this is what he was taught when he was taking the lifesaving classes five years earlier. They hammered this into him. "If you swim up to a drowning person, they will grab your head and push you under to hold themselves up." The third thought that flashed into his mind was that he knew precisely what he should do. He was not panicked or stressed. He thought to himself, *This is kind of cool. I can finally rescue a pretty girl*!

He did as he was taught. He went deeper. He pushed himself further down using her body as a ladder. He placed one hand on her waist, followed by another hand on her hips, and then her thighs, and finally to her knees. He knew drowning people never followed their rescuers underwater. When he reached her knees, he simply spun her around and climbed back up her body. This was a move he practiced many times in the pool, so everything came naturally to him. When he got back to the surface, he cradled her chin with his right hand and pushed his elbow into the middle of her back to pry her level. This maneuver is called a "chin pry" because that's exactly what it is. He kicked powerfully four or five times and moved his right hand across her left breast to her armpit and held up her weight with his right hip. Using a sidestroke, he moved her rapidly to the shallow part of the lake. She was coughing and sputtering, and her eyes were squeezed shut.

When he could finally stand in the water, he maneuvered her around so that she was cradled in his arms, much like a bride being carried over a threshold. He had finally fulfilled his destiny and saved a pretty girl from drowning.

In the meantime, Chuck had strategically maneuvered himself in the water to be right in front of Ben. Carol opened her eyes, saw Chuck standing there with his arms open, and flung herself into his arms. She was sobbing hysterically and kissing him over and over again, thanking him for saving her life. Ben just stood there, stunned. Mary Jane waded up to him and said, "That was so brave of you. Carol would have died if you hadn't rescued her." But Carol, in the meantime, kept kissing and thanking Chuck. Ben wanted to shout at her, *"You stupid bitch! I'm the one who rescued you, not Chuck. I ought to drag you back out to deep water and see how you like it."* But Chuck was his best friend, so he clenched his teeth and said nothing.

After the excitement died down, the girls decided to lie out in the sun and let their swimsuits dry off. There was no changing room, so they both put on t-shirts and shorts when it was time to leave. Ben got behind the wheel of his '58 Pontiac and Mary Jane slid across the bench seat beside him. Carol and Chuck hopped into the back seat. Off they drove with Mary Jane sitting in the middle of the front seat next to Ben, and Carol plastered right up against Chuck's side.

It was getting dark as they drove down Illinois Route 120 through the small, sleepy town of Volo. Ben could hear noises in the back seat. Carol was attempting to show Chuck how grateful she was for saving her life. Ben's eyes kept glancing up to the rearview mirror. The sound of a "Hungarian good time" drifted into his ears. He looked in the rearview mirror again, but he couldn't see them. They were both lying on that wide Pontiac bench seat.

The sounds of enthusiastic gratitude from the backseat set his hormones raging. He reached over and put his hand on Mary Jane's knee. She left it there for a moment or two, but as he began to slide his hand northward, she slapped his hand. He moved it back to her knee. They listened to WLS radio for a while and his hand slid north again, followed by the almost instantaneous slap on his hand. Not hard enough to hurt, but hard enough to let him know that she disapproved of his Admiral Byrd-like explorations. They were playing Mousetrap. He'd touch a spot on her thigh, and she would slap his hand. This continued for the next fifty miles. Mary Jane was an Irish Catholic girl, and she was in no mood to give up her honor in so tawdry a fashion. She struggled with a classic approach/avoidance conflict. He knew she was thinking to herself, *This feels good. I do want to feel closer to him. And, after all, he is a hero.* But all those years of Catholic high school and the indoctrination by the BVM (Blessed Virgin Mary or Black-Veiled Monster) nuns intervened. She would let him go a little further, but no more. He was never going to reach her "north pole."

Some hero, he thought to himself. *All that hard work, the water-logged ear infections, the frozen hair, and I can't get my hand above midthigh. Arrrgh!*

22. Saving a Life: Part II
Shit Happens

BEN DECIDED TO visit his sister on the way home from a business meeting. He wanted to show off his brand new, cobalt blue, sharkskin suit. Underneath the jacket was a crisp, white shirt with a wide, red, patterned tie. The tie was held in place by a gold tie bar emblazoned with his initials, "BC." He wore new, spit-shined black shoes. He felt he was the height of fashion on this late May day in 1970.

His sister, Mary Ann, lived in a mobile home park that, for the time, was very upscale. Her large, three-bedroom mobile home was sixty-four feet long and over twelve feet wide and was situated across the street from a picturesque retention pond. The four-acre pond was not particularly deep, but it provided a convenient resting place for Canada geese, Mallard ducks, and numerous fish that feasted upon the copious amounts of seaweed. There was a bit of green algae floating in spots near the shore as well as a few lily pads, whose small yellow flowers were just beginning to bloom. He walked up to the door, rang the bell, and again looked at the pond. Both he and his sister were mesmerized by water. They would happily sit and stare at any body of water that was bigger than a puddle. In fact, she had chosen to live in this mobile home park simply because of this pond.

She opened the door and greeted Ben with a hug and a kiss. This was customary. They were very close. And although they had squabbled together as children, as adults they both loved and respected each other. But this affection never stopped them from teasing and playfully kidding each other. Mary Ann stepped back from the embrace and said, "Damn, that's a nice suit. Is it new?"

"Yep," he replied. "Just bought it over the weekend."

"Well, it looks great!" she exclaimed. "You clean up real good!"

They went in and chatted for only a short time when Robert, her two-year-old son bounded into the room. Robert was full of the nuclear energy that all two-year-olds seem to possess. He ran up to Ben and, yanking at the sleeve of his new jacket, said, "Outside, outside! Go play!" He clearly wanted to play outside. So, Ben, being the dutiful uncle that he was, said, "Sure, Robert. Let's go for a walk." After all, it was a warm day with a bright blue sky and just a few puffy, white clouds. Numerous lilac bushes located in the park added a sweet fragrance to the soft breeze.

Ben and Robert walked next to each other down the deserted side street that encircled the pond. Robert pointed to the pond and said, "Water!"

"Yes," Ben said, "Water!"

Robert said, even louder, "WATER!" and immediately jumped over the curb and ran full speed to the pond. Ben stood there and watched, reasoning that Robert lived here and would know to stop at the edge of the pond. Apparently, he didn't.

In fact, Robert sprinted into the pond like a pint-sized track star. His momentum carried him about ten feet from the shore. Although the pond was not very deep, it was certainly over his head. He stopped running and he just floated, arms out, face down.

Ben froze for a moment, somehow hoping that

Robert would turn around and swim to shore, which he realized was ridiculous. He had no choice but to go into the pond after him. The bottom of the pond was muddy and sucked at his shoes. He reached Robert and pulled him up onto his left shoulder. At this point, the water was chest-deep, just covering Ben's tie bar. Robert immediately started screaming and crying. When Ben heard the cries, he knew that Robert would be fine. No need for artificial resuscitation or anything like that. Ben turned in the pond and headed back through the algae and lily pads to the shore. However, as he turned his left shoe got sucked into the muck and began its journey to the center of the earth. Ben staggered up onto the shore, feeling that the adventure was now over. Unfortunately, he was wrong.

There is a rather common expression that is frequently used figuratively: "Scare the shit out of you." In Robert's case, this expression became literal. His totally soaked diaper did little to contain the bursting dam of effluence that now dripped down the side of Ben's new suit jacket, cascaded down his left pant leg, and onto his stocking-clad left foot. In many ways, it's quite amazing how much shit a two-year-old little boy can expel. Perhaps because it was mixed with urine and algae-infested pond water as well, it somehow expanded the volume. At this point, at least the top of Ben's jacket was still clean. But Robert's crying led to a runny nose, complete with snot bubbles, which now decorated his left shoulder. *Oh well. Might as well get EVERY bodily fluid out of Robert and on to my new suit. At least he didn't puke.*

It was hard to describe the smell. The muck on the bottom of ponds frequently releases methane and other gasses which have their own foul odor. The perfume of the algae combines with and enhances this aroma. While the feces and urine add just enough spice to make one's eyes water.

Robert continued to scream, which caused Mary Ann to run out of her front door. She ran down the four steps to her driveway and her jaw dropped. Ben was walking toward her covered in seaweed, mud, algae, urine, snot, and shit. She stood there in shock. His right shoe squeaked as water oozed out through the shoelaces. His left foot made a wet slapping sound as it touched down on the pavement. She realized her son was OK and began to laugh. Once she started, she could not stop. She laughed harder and harder until she could no longer stand. Doubled over, she plopped down on her butt on the driveway and just laughed.

Ben dripped his way over to her and tried to explain what had happened. But all she could do was hold up her hand in a motion to stop and laugh. Tears streamed down her face and she struggled to catch her breath.

"Yeah, right. Real fucking funny!" is all Ben managed to say.

She took Robert from him, ran to the house, threw him into the bathtub and washed him off and put him in clean clothes. Robert had quieted down seeing his mother and was obviously no worse for wear. Ben plopped on the front step. He stayed there just thinking and stinking. *Now what the hell do I do?*

Mary Ann came out after she got Robert settled down and decided the only thing they could do for Ben was to spray him down with the garden hose. Ben originally thought, *Wait a minute, the water will ruin my suit. It's supposed to be dry-cleaned.* Then he realized how stupid that was. It was way too late for that.

Mary Ann gleefully hosed down her brother like he was an old Buick. Once the great majority of the human and pond filth had been removed, they debated as to what to do next. Finally, she decided that the best approach was for her to get a large beach towel and for him to strip underneath it. She took all the washable clothes from him and threw them in her washing machine. The suit pants and jacket, along with the tie, were placed in a garbage bag. Later they would be brought to the cleaners where the horrified old Asian woman reluctantly took them, swearing under her breath in what sounded like Chinese. Surprisingly the pants and jacket came out fine. But, alas, the red tie shriveled up like a dead gecko's tongue and was a total loss.

Meanwhile, Ben hopped into the shower. When he dried off, he put on one of her husband's robes. Somehow, he felt exhausted. Saving Robert's life had expended very little physical energy. But the emotional experience just drained him. He plopped down in the recliner chair in the living room. They had just begun to talk when her husband, Darryl, showed up. The sight that greeted him was an obviously naked man, wearing his robe, sitting in his recliner, talking to his wife.

Now Darryl was the toughest son-of-a-bitch

that Ben or his sister had ever met. His biography read like a cheap dime-store novel. He worked riverboats on the Mississippi, rodeos in Texas, owned a carnival, and fought in the Korean War until he got blown up so badly that he only regained consciousness after he was hospitalized in Japan. He somehow enjoyed combat enough that he volunteered to go back to Korea, but the army decided he had had enough and sent him home. He wasn't a particularly big man – about average height, but lean and rangy. The blood vessels bulged in his forearms. He just had the look about him that said, "You can fuck with me, but I will kill you."

As he saw Ben sitting there, he clenched his fist and got ready to pounce, much like a leopard would prepare to kill an antelope.

"WHAT THE HELL IS GOIN' ON HERE?!" Darryl bellowed.

Just when things looked like they would turn violent, the thought entered Darryl's brain, *Wait a minute, that's her brother.* His intense stare and furrowed eyebrows relaxed into a comically, quizzical look.

In a much softer and confused tone, Darryl repeated, "What the hell is goin' on here?" At which point Mary Ann began laughing again. And to make matters worse, so did Ben. Neither one could explain what had happened because they were laughing so hard. Mary Ann eventually sputtered out a few barely intelligible words, including "Robert" and "the pond."

When Ben's clothes eventually dried, he got dressed, borrowed a pair of Darryl's jeans, and drove home with his one shoe. Fortunately, it was his right shoe, so it was easy to press on the gas and brake. As he headed east down Irving Park Rd., he thought to himself, *Hey, I've now saved two people from drowning. All that training made me a hero. A big, fucking hero.* And he began to laugh.

23. Picture This: Part I
I See Dead People (and they're naked)

CARRIE WAS A cute cop. Brown hair, big brown eyes, and a pixie-like face that made her look younger than her years. Because of her friendly demeanor and ready smile, if you met her on the street out of uniform, she didn't look like a cop. She looked more like an elementary school teacher, or perhaps a nurse. But, her way of talking, combined with a colorful vocabulary, made her seem like "one of the guys." She was a down-to-earth woman who had no time or patience for the "prissy."

When Carrie was younger, she wanted to be a photographer. And so, she went to the local community college to study photography. While there, she needed to fill her schedule with other courses and, randomly, picked a criminal justice course. It changed her life. While she still loved photography, she slowly realized it would be very hard to make a living in that profession. She would probably be stuck taking pictures of families for their personalized Christmas cards. The dreams of working for *National Geographic* seemed as unrealistic as the dreams of little boys hoping to play in the NBA.

Carrie completed every course that was offered at the community college involving criminal justice. She worked hard. Not only mentally to get an "A" in almost every class she was in, but also physically. To be accepted into a police department, she had to pass rigorous physical fitness tests, including running a timed mile. Cigarettes were not her friend in this matter. But she persevered. She had found her career.

Being a police officer is hard, frequently boring, and occasionally terrifying. So naturally, she wanted more, and she found it on TV. At that time, it was hard not to watch CSI (crime scene investigation) shows. They were in New York, Miami, and Las Vegas. Later on, they even created a cyber division. Each episode highlighted extremely well-equipped labs and all sorts of futuristic equipment. They solved crime after crime and Carrie wanted in. She took evidence technician classes at the State Police Academy and eventually earned her certification in that field. Her main job was to photograph, in tremendous detail, both real and suspected crime scenes.

The town in which she worked was relatively peaceful, so Carrie began to work part-time for a county-wide law enforcement group. When needed, she would be called to document evidence at crime scenes throughout the suburban area. This brought about more money and the opportunity to use her photographic skills in ways she had never foreseen. It also brought her to unexpected scenarios.

Spoiler alert: old people die! While it is true that some die in hospitals or in car accidents, very few actually die because of criminal activity. But you never know. So, the crime scene photographer must document every location where a dead body is discovered. Second spoiler alert: a lot of elderly people die at home! This makes sense because as people age, they go out less and less. And according to Carrie, a surprising number die in bed or on the toilet seat. And, they are naked. So much for leading the glamorous life of *CSI: Miami*.

On rare occasions, elderly people are murdered, and, in some cases, it is made to look like they died of natural causes. So, when a person dies at home, people like Carrie have to document the scene in tremendous detail, in case foul play is discovered later.

It is not always easy to tell when a person is dead. They may have suffered a stroke, fallen into a coma, or become unconscious for a variety of reasons. In many towns, the police cannot decide that the naked person who is lying in bed, unmoving, is "really most sincerely dead." So, the towns require that CPR be started and maintained until the paramedics arrive. This policy is for the safety of the allegedly dead and to keep the vultures...ahem...lawyers, away.

★ ★ ★

CARRIE AND HER partner, Frank, arrived at a typical bi-level home. They were responding to a 911 call from a neighbor and were first on the scene because they had been only two blocks away when the call came. All they knew was that there was an unresponsive man at this location who had been found by his neighbor. The neighbor greeted them in the driveway. She was crying and said, "I went to check on him because

CAPTAIN BILLY C.

I hadn't seen him, and he hadn't picked up his newspaper. He's upstairs in the bedroom and he's not moving. I think he's dead."

Officer Frank said, "The paramedics are on their way. They should be here in a few minutes. Please wait outside while we check on him."

Carrie and Frank rapidly moved into the man's home, looked around to make sure no one else was in the house, ran up the five stairs to the bedroom, and saw the man face up on the bed. And, as usual, he was naked. He was old, mostly bald, with bushy eyebrows and a shaggy gray mustache above his open mouth. He was very overweight and there was silver hair covering most of his body. Frank immediately checked for his pulse and could find none. His chest lacked the rise and fall of the living. They were pretty sure he was dead, but procedure required them to start CPR. They knew they could not do CPR on a bed because the chest compressions would lose their efficiency on the soft mattress.

"I'll take the top half. It's heavier and I wouldn't want a pretty little girl like you hurting her back moving Shamu over here," Frank said, gesturing at the corpulent corpse.

Carrie knew he was joking and appreciated

his gallantry but responded in the only way appropriate to the situation. "Fuck you, asshole!" She gave him a dirty look, but there was a twinkle in her eye. They had played games like this often.

After putting on his disposable gloves, Frank slid his hands under the man's shoulders and grunted. Carrie donned her gloves and grabbed the man by his ankles. They counted to three but could not lift his supine body off the bed. So, they slid him to the side of the bed and used all their strength to prevent gravity from damaging him any further. They barely got him to the floor without dropping him or banging his head on the tile.

In the process of moving him, Carrie's phone that she had tucked into her shirt pocket fell out and landed on the man's dick. (I apologize for using the word "dick" rather than "penis," but as I described earlier, Carrie has a colorful vocabulary) Before she could retrieve her phone, his bladder muscles relaxed, and he peed on it. Long and hard. So hard, she jerked back to avoid being splashed. Then she knelt and stared at her newly baptized iPhone. Frank started laughing. He choked out, "Oh well, April showers."

This time she meant it. "Fuck you, asshole!

CAPTAIN BILLY C.

That's a new phone!"

At this point, the paramedics arrived, barging into the room with their hundreds of pounds of equipment. They were followed by a gaggle of firemen with yet more equipment. Carrie grabbed one of the paramedics and said, "Give me your Sani-wipes."

The paramedic looked puzzled and asked, "What for?"

"Shut up. Just give them to me."

Not being a dull person, the paramedic sensed that she was in no mood for conversation and handed her the container. She retrieved her phone from the man's dick and began wiping it off. The paramedics attached the AED (automatic electronic defibrillator) pad to the man's chest.

Carrie walked out of the increasingly crowded bedroom, stared down at her iPhone, and said, "Hey, Frank! It still works!" She playfully put the phone up to her ear and asked, "Can you hear me now?!"

24. Picture This: Part II
The Great Wall of Fred

CARRIE AND FRANK arrived at the scene in separate cars, each called in by the county to document evidence surrounding the death of an elderly gentleman. The paramedics had arrived before them and were loading most of their equipment back into their ambulance. Curiously, the Sawzall was sitting next to the front stoop of the house with several firemen standing around it, talking about the Cubs. The only other thing left out was a wheeled stretcher, with a neatly folded body bag on top. There were several squad cars parked haphazardly, and most of the police officers were talking and joking with each other.

Carrie grabbed her camera bag, greeted Frank, and asked, "What's up?"

Frank shrugged his shoulders. "Don't know. Just got a call on my cell phone from the county to show up and document the scene."

"Yeah, well, me too," Carrie responded.

CAPTAIN BILLY C.

"Have you seen the Sarge?" Frank asked as he scanned the gathering.

"No, I haven't," Carrie replied, looking around. "Oh, there he is. He's by the front door. I guess we'd better get over there and find out what's up."

"Hey, Sarge. What's the story?" Frank asked as they walked up to the sergeant.

The sergeant nodded at Frank and Carrie. He paused and said, "Well, this is a strange one. As near as we can figure, a man by the name of Fred McNamara died of natural causes several days ago. And, because of certain circumstances, we'd better do a good job of documenting this."

"Circumstances, Sarge?" Carrie questioned.

The sergeant scratched his head. "It seems that his nephew discovered Mr. McNamara this morning when he came to check on him. When we got the call, we checked our records and discovered that Mr. McNamara had filed several complaints with the department saying that his neighbors were too noisy, and he couldn't sleep. We came out several times, but the neighbors were just watching television, and when we arrived it really wasn't loud. Mr. McNamara insisted, however, that they raised such a racket that he could not sleep. So, he took matters into his own hands."

"What did he do?" asked Frank.

"I think it's better I show you rather than tell you. You're going to love this. Follow me. By the way, like I said, it's been a couple of days. You might want to put on your masks – it's really ripe in there."

"Great!" moaned Carrie, as she and Frank both put on their masks. Carrie took a small container of Vick's VapoRub out of her bag. She opened it up and put a small blob of it on her mask under her nose. "Maybe this will help," Carrie said, as she offered some to Frank and he did the same.

They followed the Sarge into the small ranch house that pretty much looked like all the other small ranch houses in the neighborhood. The exterior was red brick, with a little stonework in the front under the picture window. A narrow driveway led to a two-car garage in the back. There was the "mandatory" chain-link fence surrounding the backyard.

Sarge guided them to a bedroom, stood outside next to the door, jerked his thumb toward the room, and said, "He's in there."

Carrie turned the corner and walked through the door. "What the fuck?" she blurted as she stopped abruptly.

Frank, who was right behind her, collided with her back. "Sorry," he said.

Carrie stopped because there was a wooden wall that was over six feet tall right inside the bedroom door. As she looked around, she realized there was a walled-off area inside the extremely cramped bedroom. As she explored further, she followed a narrow little walkway to an opening in the wall that was just big enough for a person to squeeze in sideways to get to the bed. The wall completely surrounded the bed. She and Frank immediately stepped out of the bedroom and said, in unison, "What the...?"

The Sarge started laughing. Frank and Carrie waited, impatiently. Finally, the sergeant choked, "Well..." He stopped and had to clear his throat. "Well, according to the nephew, Mr. McNamara in there," gesturing with his thumb, "couldn't stand the noise any longer and decided to build the wall around his bed to keep out the noise."

Frank asked, "Why the fuck didn't he just use earplugs?"

"You'd have to ask him," the Sarge replied.

"And he ain't talking."

"What do you want us to do?" Carrie asked.

The Sarge replied, "Take as many pictures as you can to document whatever this is. When you're done, the firemen will take down a section of the wall so they can get Mr. McNamara out of Fort Apache."

Carrie and Frank side-slithered into the room to see how they could get pictures. Carrie said to Frank, "Look, I can't get enough distance from anywhere inside the wall to take the type of pictures I need. I'm not sure what to do now. Let's get out of this sewer pit of a room and figure out what our game plan is."

They stared at the wall from the doorway and Frank said, "You know, for a crazy person, this guy wasn't a bad carpenter. That wall looks pretty sturdy. And if you look, he tried his best to insulate it from sound using any piece of Styrofoam he could find and stuffing it between the two by fours. There's even some old egg cartons stapled to the wall." They both stared at the wall in silence, admiring Mr. McNamara's homage to a similar construction project in China.

Finally, Carrie said, "You know, if I get on top of the wall, I can shoot down and have enough

CAPTAIN BILLY C.

distance to get the shots that I need."

Frank asked, "How are you going to get up there?"

"There's an old nightstand in the corner. If I climb up on top of that, I might be able to lean over the wall enough to get some shots."

Frank dragged the nightstand to where he thought the foot of the bed would be. And with a little help from Frank, Carrie struggled to stand on the nightstand. The climb and the position were awkward. It was a narrow space and there wasn't as much room as she thought between the wall and the ceiling. She looked at Frank and said, "Listen, I'm going to have to lean way over to take some pictures. I need you to hold on to my belt to keep me from falling on 'Dead Fred' over there." With that, she pulled herself up and slithered forward until her abdomen was resting on the top of the wall and holding all her weight, her feet dangling in midair. Frank got behind her as close as he could and held her belt to keep her from falling, his face right next to her ass.

Carrie yelled at him, "If you pull down my pants while I am hanging over this wall, I want to remind you that I have a gun, and I know how to use it!" Frank laughed.

Having her pants pulled down by Frank wasn't Carrie's biggest fear. She was afraid she would lean too far forward and fall face-first onto the corpse. She was also afraid that the increased pressure on her lower abdomen would cause her to fart right in Frank's face. And she certainly didn't want that embarrassment. Although, she reasoned, if it was "silent, but deadly" he might not notice.

He might not notice because the smell inside the room, and even more so inside the wall, was horrid. It smelled like rotten eggs or sulfur with a tinge of stale urine and feces. The mask helped, but not enough. She looked through her camera and began to focus on the man. His skin glistened with a pale sheen and had a greenish tint. He was beginning to bloat. His eyes were bulging out of their sockets and his tongue protruded from his mouth. A truly grotesque picture! She began to snap away.

A few minutes later, she called to Frank. "OK, I've got what I need from here. Pull me down before I puke!" He tugged on her belt and she slid down with Frank guiding her foot to the nightstand and from there jumped to the floor. She took a few more pictures of the wall and the little opening to the bed. Then she and Frank headed outside.

As they stepped outside, they took off their masks and sucked in fresh air. Carrie told one of the firemen, "He's all yours." She watched as he picked up the Sawzall and headed into the bedroom.

"You know," she said to Frank, "I could have been a wildlife photographer for *National Geographic*. Or maybe even a paparazzi at the Cannes Film Festival. But I chose this glamorous career instead. *Crime Scene Investigations*, my ass! I gotta go take a shower!"

"Me too," said Frank. "Me too."

25. Much Ado About Nothing

THEY STARED AT each other from across the multi-purpose room. Then they looked away. Slowly, they both moved to the left, not looking directly at each other, but keenly aware of the other's presence. While moving to the left, they also moved forward, closing the distance between them. To the casual observer, nothing was amiss. Again, they moved, spiraling ever closer to the center of the room; like stars being drawn into the violent abyss of a black hole. Seconds ticked by. The tension mounted. They locked eyes, froze in place, and then sprang toward each other like two predators locked in mortal combat. They snarled and grabbed each other's hair, continuing their spinning around, knocking over chairs and tables, and finally crashing to the floor.

The staff immediately dropped what they were doing and ran over to try, unsuccessfully, to pull the two combatants apart. More staff were summoned, and raced to the center of the room, finally separating them. Vulgarities and spittle flew towards their opponent as the two were dragged to opposite corners and forced to sit down, where they continued to fume and swear. The police were called.

★ ★ ★

Principal Jan Schmidt stood in the doorway, looking at Bruce LaBonte, her Dean of Students, who sat in his chair, rubbing his knee. "Are you OK, Bruce?" she asked. "I heard you took quite a tumble breaking up the fight."

"Yeah, I guess so. I've been hurt worse."

Jan stepped into Bruce's office and closed the door. She sat in the chair next to his desk. "Bruce, if you want to go to the emergency room to get your knee x-rayed, the school district will pay for it. It's all part of worker's comp, you know."

Bruce, still rubbing his knee, replied, "I'm sure it will be OK. But thanks."

"What started the fight, anyway?"

"I talked to the two girls. Maria Lopez is a new student and she said she doesn't even know Jessica. Jessica, for her part, said that Maria, and I'm going to quote here, 'was looking at me all hard and shit, so I had no choice.' I suspended them both, and their moms will pick them up in a few minutes. I'll talk to both sets of parents and see if we can straighten this out."

Jan nodded. "I'll be back shortly with some forms for you to sign. The district requires that anytime there is an injury," Jan used air quotes, "'in the line of duty' a detailed explanation must be submitted. I'll have to see if I can find the forms. We don't normally have much use for them here." She paused and added, "Maybe you'll get a purple heart to match your purple knee."

"Very funny, boss."

As soon as she stood up to leave, there was a knock on the door. Cheryl, Bruce's secretary, stepped in and said, "I hate to interrupt this, but the Michigan City, IN police are on the phone wanting to talk to you immediately. They're on line two."

Bruce's face turned white. He immediately picked up the phone and punched the button for line two. Jan sat back down. She cared about Bruce and could see that something was wrong. Also, she was very curious why a police department one hundred miles away would be calling

CAPTAIN BILLY C.

her Dean of Students.

Bruce said, into the phone, "You're kidding, right? ... Is she OK? ... I suppose I could get there, but it will take me over two hours... Have you tried reaching my sister? She lives in Michigan City... No, she wouldn't be home now. But she should answer her cell phone...No, that's not it. Let me give you the correct number. It's 219-871-5386... no, 86...If you can't reach her, call me back and I'll leave immediately."

Jan looked at Bruce, expectantly.

"Boss, you're not going to believe this. My mom just got into a fight with another woman at the adult daycare facility. Apparently, it was quite the brawl."

"Is she OK?"

"Yeah, she's fine. But someone has to pick her up because the police and the facility don't want her there. She's been suspended! If they can't locate my sister, I'm going to have to take the afternoon off and go get her. And by the time I get to the Indiana border, 294 is going to be backed up."

Jan quizzically looked at Bruce. "I'm a little confused. What's an adult daycare center?"

Bruce went back to rubbing his knee with

much more agitated energy than before. He replied, "My mom has Alzheimer's and it's getting worse. There's a variety of services available for people like my mom. She lives with my sister, but during the day she drops her off at adult daycare, which is the exact same thing moms do for little children. This gives my sister a break during the day. Otherwise, taking care of my mom would simply wear her out. The next step would be a memory unit at an assisted living facility. She would be there 24-7. Those units are locked to keep the residents from walking out the door. Many Alzheimer's patients have a tendency to wander and it would be very easy for them to get lost or hurt. Obviously, assisted living costs a lot more, so we're trying to keep her at home as long as we can. The adult daycare allows us to do that. For now."

Jan stood to leave again and said, "Please let me know how things work out with your mom. Two fights in one day, can you believe it? Must be a full moon! I see Jessica's mom just came in. I'll take care of Mohammed Ali. You and your sister deal with Sonny Liston"

★ ★ ★

CAPTAIN BILLY C.

LATER THAT EVENING, Bruce and his sister, Joanne, spoke on the phone.

"What did the adult daycare facility say caused this brawl," Bruce asked.

Joanne laughed. "According to the staff, no one knows. They said it was just two old, crazy, Italian women trying to beat the hell out of each other. Probably over some guy they both saw and liked."

Bruce scratched his head. "Do you know who the other woman was?"

"Not really. She's rather new to the facility. I don't know that much about her."

There was a moment of silence as Bruce grew concerned. "Has mom been kicked out of the facility, or just suspended for a few days? And what about the police?"

Joanne replied, "The good news is she's not expelled, and she can go back on Monday. The other good news is the police can't figure out how they would press charges against two 80 something-year-old women with Alzheimer's for getting into a fistfight. But the facility had to file a report to protect itself."

"And nobody's hurt, right?"

Joanne replied, "No, amazingly they're both

fine. They both could have wound up with broken hips or shoulders or God only knows what else. But, they're both fine."

"Damn, we dodged a bullet on this one."

"There is some bad news, though. I was trying to trim mom's nails when I got her home, but she stopped me. She said, 'I need to leave them long so I can gouge that bitch's eyes out.' Bruce, I don't know how much longer I can handle her. I think it's time we consider assisted living. I've already talked to our brother Tom and he agrees."

Bruce sighed heavily. "I suppose you're right. You've done an amazing job taking care of her these last few years, but it's probably time. What's the name of that facility we both liked in LaPorte – the one with the memory care unit? You know, it had all the finches in the glass enclosure in the lobby. I think mom would be happy there."

★ ★ ★

THREE MONTHS LATER, Bruce sat in the school cafeteria, eating his rubber chicken, and watching Jessica and Maria sitting next to each other, talking and laughing. Apparently, the two pugilists had more than reconciled their differences. He stood up, walked to the garbage can, scraped his plate of the residue of the totally unsatisfactory lunch, stacked his tray on the counter, and headed to his office. Seeing Jessica and Maria together reminded him that he needed to call his sister to find out how his mom was doing.

Once he was back in his office, he called his sister. "Joanne, how's mom?"

She responded, "I just got back from LaPorte. You're not going to believe this. You know that old 'dago' lady that mom was fighting with? She is now in residence, just down the hall from mom."

"Oh, shit," Bruce slapped his forehead with the heel of his hand.

Joanne continued, "Apparently, they recognized each other as someone they knew, but didn't remember they were enemies. So now, they are wandering the halls together, arm in arm. I guess it was much ado about nothing."

Bruce thought a minute and replied, "Seems like there's a lot of that going around."

26. Justice is Blind

STACY STOOD IN front of her closet. She was having a hard time deciding which outfit to wear to go to court. She eventually decided on a bright blue short-sleeved shell with a deeply cut V-neck. It would go well with the tight white jeans she had already chosen.

Stacy was a short, thin girl with a vastly oversized bosom for someone so young and so thin. Most men thought that thirty pounds of her one-hundred-pound weight was located in her chest and marveled that she could remain upright. She put on the shell and looked at herself in the mirror. The electric blue top combined with the form-fitting jeans was stunning enough, but the plunging V-neck showed off her cleavage which seemed to go on forever. She added a necklace with a sparkly rhinestone, heart-shaped pendant just to make sure everyone's eyes would be drawn to the right area. She added a touch of perfume behind each ear and a dab between her breasts. Her bright red hair framed her alabaster face, and her full lips, which usually showed a subtle pout, just begged to be kissed.

With looks like these, it would be easy to assume that Stacy was promiscuous. But nothing could be further from the truth. She didn't need to have sex with boys to get their attention. With her looks and, if necessary, a subtle hint, she could get whatever she wanted from boys without ever having to succumb to their desires. She remembered what her mother had told her long ago, "Men are like babies. If you jangle keys in front of infants, they go goofy. They squirm and giggle and smile. Their hands and their feet kick randomly in their excitement. This is what boys and men do when they see a sexy girl. They can't help it. It's just their nature."

Stacy knew this was true. She remembered walking in front of the school on a warm day in May and watching a boy run by her. He turned to stare at her chest and ran into a light pole, breaking his nose. He had to go to the emergency room to have his nose re-set. She laughed. He must have had a hard time explaining to his mother why he ran into the pole. She also remembered one of the fathers staring at her while attempting to pick his son up from the school. The man drove up onto the curb and almost hit Mrs. Wolfe, the science teacher. Mrs. Wolfe, the disciplinarian that she was, wasted no time chastising the man in front of an audience of smirking students.

At fifteen, Stacy looked a lot like her thirty-three-year-old mother. She and her mother, Tracy, were equally flirtatious and her mother was sure they could pass for sisters. They often shared clothes and Stacy wasn't sure if the bright blue shell was hers or her mother's.

Stacy was positive that the judge would be lenient once he got a good look at her. In 1981, female judges were rare so she was confident that, as usual, she would get what she wanted.

★ ★ ★

"WELL, YOU LOOK spiffy this morning. Secret job interview?" Sandi asked Bryan as he came into the kitchen.

"No, remember I've got to go to court today," Bryan said as he stirred his coffee.

"What'd they accuse you of this time?"

"Nothing. It's the truancy case I told you

about."

"Aren't you a little old to be charged with truancy? I thought they might have gotten you for that overdue library book. Or blasting *Born to Be Wild* in your car, rattling everybody's windows."

"Actually, this is important. It's the first time we've brought a truancy case to the local court."

"I remember you telling me about the town passing a truancy law and I could never understand why they bothered. Isn't it exactly the same as the state law?" Sandi asked.

"It is. Word for word."

"So why did the town pass a law that already existed?"

"Allow me to enlighten you. Illinois has had a truancy law for generations. But for the over four million people living in Cook County, which covers all of Chicago and many of its suburbs, how many truancy officers do you think they have?"

"I would guess a couple hundred."

"And you would be very wrong. The answer is, one."

"One? You've got to be kidding me."

"Nope, just one. Some of the poorer, inner-city

schools could probably use a truant officer for just their building. So, I, along with a whole bunch of other people, pushed the town to pass a law so that it could be locally enforced, and school resource officers can write tickets that require the parent and student to appear in court. The town partially did it to cut down on the crime rate."

"Wait, what?"

"If you watch TV news, most people get the impression that burglaries are committed by either highly skilled criminals or drug-crazed gang members breaking down your door in a nighttime home invasion. In reality, most burglaries are committed by teenagers in the middle of the day when no one is home. If the teenagers are all in school, the number of burglaries drops. If they're cutting school and wandering around unsupervised, they tend to get in trouble. So, that's why there's the new law. And this is the first case."

"So, who is this dastardly perpetrator?"

"Stacy."

"Stacy?"

"You remember, the girl I told you about with the titanic tits?"

"Oh, that Stacy. Why did she miss so much

school?"

"Well, I asked her, and she said, 'I don't need school.' I pointed out to her that almost every career requires a high school diploma. She said, 'Mine doesn't. I want to work as a coat-check girl at one of the big clubs in Chicago.' She then leaned forward, showing off her boobs, and asked, 'Do you have any idea how much money a girl like me can make in tips working as a coat-check girl?' I was so shocked; I didn't know what to say. She smiled and winked at me and left my office. She continued to miss a lot of school, so I had Paul Pulaski, the school cop, write her a ticket." Bryan looked at his watch and said, "Hey, I'd better get going. Don't want to be late for the biggest trial since Charlie Manson's *Helter Skelter*."

★ ★ ★

PAUL SAW BRYAN enter the back of the courtroom and motioned to him to come to the front and stand on the right side with the other police officers. "Might as well stand here. You get a better view of the proceedings. And they tolerate us talking a little more than they do in the gallery.

We've got Rick Romero as the judge today. This guy is amazingly bright and…"

"All rise. The Honorable Richard Romero presiding," the bailiff called out. And with that, he led the judge to his chair behind the imposing bench.

Judge Romero said, "Be seated."

Paul whispered in Bryan's ear, "And he is blind as a bat."

Bryan looked around the courtroom. He did not see Stacy or her mother. But as everyone settled down, and the first case was called, the pair made their entrance with their usual flair and, stylishly late, sashayed their way to the front of the court. Everyone stared and several men stood and stumbled to the side to make room for them.

What followed were several cases involving petty infractions of the law: speeding, running a red light, shoplifting, and the more serious crime of drunk driving. The judge handled each case efficiently, asking clarifying questions only when needed. It was easy to forget he was blind. Or in Stacy's case, never to even notice.

When Stacy's name was called, she and her mother stood to the left in front of the bench while Bryan and Paul stood on the right with the prosecuting attorney. The attorney said, "Your honor, this is a case involving truancy. The defendant is fifteen and is accused of missing numerous days of school..."

The judge interrupted and said, "Counselor, let's push this case back to the end of the morning. Given the defendant's age, I would prefer to do it once most of the court has been cleared."

The attorney said, "Very well, your honor." Stacy and her mom both rolled their eyes and sighed heavily with exasperation, realizing their whole morning was shot. In the meantime, everyone went back to their previous locations.

More cases followed and everything seemed to be humming along like a well-oiled machine. That is until a middle-aged man appeared in front of the judge and caused everything to grind to a halt. When asked how he pleaded, the man responded in a high-pitched, overly loud, inarticulate voice, "Naught gurity." The man then began speaking and signing to the judge. No one in the court had the foggiest notion as to what the man was saying.

Judge Romero turned to the bailiff and asked, "Bailiff, what is going on here?"

"Your honor, it appears the man before you is deaf. And he is attempting to sign to you."

Judge Romero said, "Well, that's not going to work out. Did he bring anyone else with him who can read sign language?"

The prosecuting attorney turned and put his hand on the shoulder of the defendant to get his attention. Then, hoping that if he spoke loud enough the deaf man could miraculously hear him, he practically shouted, "Did you bring anyone with you? Someone who can read sign language?"

The deaf defendant, having read the prosecutor's lips, nodded his head vigorously, turned around, and signed toward someone in the back of the gallery. A man stood up and walked briskly to the front of the courtroom. The two men signed to each other franticly. The hope was that the defendant's companion would act as an interpreter. But that hope was quickly dashed on the rocky shore of reality. Both men were deaf and neither one could speak clearly. They knew what each other was signing but could not make themselves understood to the judge or the prosecuting attorney.

Once this was explained to the judge, the bailiff interjected, "Well, maybe they could call someone."

The judge jerked his head toward the bailiff in a blind double-take and asked, "How would they know if someone answered?" The bailiff shrugged his shoulders and blushed. Judge Romero then asked the prosecuting attorney, "What is this man accused of?"

The prosecuting attorney looked to the police officer standing next to him and asked, "Officer Plunkett?"

The policeman said, "Failure to come to a complete stop at a stop sign, your honor."

The judge let out with an exasperated sigh. "Are you telling me, Officer Plunkett, that you gave a ticket to a deaf man for running a stop sign?"

"Uh, yes, your honor."

"Interesting. Let's move this case to the end of the morning session along with the truancy case. Any objections to this move?" the judge asked in exasperation.

"Uh, no, your honor."

When Officer Plunkett rejoined the other cops at the side of the court, he immediately began taking abuse from his cohorts.

"Nice going, Barney Fife."

"What's next? A jaywalking ticket to an old lady on crutches?"

"How about a parking ticket for a guy in a wheelchair?"

"Guys, guys, I couldn't help it. I thought he was screwing around. I didn't know if he was drunk, high, or stupid, and I started writing the ticket because I was pissed. Once I started, I realized he was deaf, but by then I had to finish filling it out."

Being the kind, gentle police officers his friends were, they cut him absolutely no slack and continued making fun out of him as best they could without causing a disturbance and pissing off the judge even further.

The court resumed humming along and gradually emptied until there were only a few people left. The bailiff said to the judge, "Your honor, there are only two cases left. Which would you like first?"

Judge Romero commanded, "Let's do the stop sign first."

The bailiff motioned to the deaf men to come forward. The two gentlemen walked to the front of the court.

CAPTAIN BILLY C.

The judge "looked" at the police officer. Obviously, a blind person cannot "look" at an individual, but Judge Romero had an uncanny ability to know exactly where everyone was in the courtroom at all times. He would turn to a speaker to ask them questions, giving the impression to a casual observer that he was, indeed, looking at them. Or, in this case, glaring at them.

"Officer Plunkett, do you believe that the defendant has suffered enough for his dastardly crime of failing to come to a complete stop at a stop sign?"

"Oh, yes, your honor, yes. I think he has suffered more than enough."

"Very well, officer. Case dismissed. Bailiff, please make sure that the defendant knows he is free to go with no prejudice or fines."

Seeing no other defendants in the courtroom, Stacy and her mother walked to the front. Bryan Costello and Paul Pulaski walked up as well and stood next to the prosecuting attorney. The bailiff swore in Bryan and Officer Pulaski as well as Stacy and her mother.

Judge Romero asked the prosecuting attorney, "Can you give me a brief synopsis of what this case is about?"

THE BEST LAID PLANS...

"Your honor, I believe Mr. Costello, from High School District 224, would be a better choice for summarizing this case. Mr. Costello…"

"Your honor, in the past quarter, or forty-five school days, Stacy Dowd has missed twenty-one full days and eight half days. Your honor, she is only fifteen and in spite of letters and repeated phone calls to her mother, Stacy has chosen not to attend school."

The judge turned toward Stacy and asked, "Miss Dowd, do you suffer from a medical condition that prevents you from going to school?"

Stacy pointlessly wiggled her body and replied, "Well…"

"Miss Dowd, may I remind you that you are under oath and any health issue must be verifiable by a medical professional."

"Well…in that case, no, your honor." Stacy subtly pulled her shell down by the hem, lowering the neckline.

Stacy and her mother looked confused. They had both leaned forward hoping to show off their cleavage, obviously oblivious to the fact that the judge was blind. The mom began to fuss with her hair, hoping the judge would notice. Stacy put both hands behind her back and pivoted seductively side to side. Their actions looked more pitiful than erotic.

The judge then asked, "Is there any reason that you did not attend school?"

"Your honor, it's so B-O-R-I-N-G," she whined.

"Please understand – boring is not a defense. Mrs. Dowd, do you have any explanation for your daughter's behavior?"

"I told her to go to school, your honor, but she just doesn't listen." Tracy threw back her shoulders as she spoke, sticking out her breasts.

"Very well, perhaps she needs an incentive to listen. I'm levying a one-hundred-dollar fine that I will temporarily suspend. And I order you to appear in court at the end of the school year in June. If your attendance has improved dramatically, I will waive the fine and dismiss the charge. If, however, Mr. Costello comes back to court and tells me you have missed school, I will add a fine of twenty-five dollars for every day you have missed. Bailiff, please schedule a court date on my first open calendar date in June." The judge banged his gavel and said, "Court is adjourned."

As they walked out of the courtroom, Stacy

and her mother looked at each other. Stacy said, "I really thought this killer outfit would work."

Her mother snarled bitterly, "Apparently, sometimes justice IS blind."

27. Send in the Clowns – Don't Bother, They're Here

"Geez, you look terrible! What the hell happened to you?" Christine asked.

"I've been broiling in the sun since one o'clock," responded Butch, "and I've got to pee. Watch all the blankets!"

"All right, all right. Don't be such a wuss!" retorted Jim.

Jim and Christine looked at each other as Butch walked away. "What time did he say he got here?" asked Christine.

"One o'clock."

"He's been sitting out here in the sun for the past four and a half hours?! No wonder he's crabby!"

Jim guffawed, "He really does look sunburned. He looks like a mascot for Red Lobster!"

"I can't believe he's been sitting here for four and a half hours."

Jim replied, "He's been whining about this

concert since they announced it back in February. He bullied six of us into buying tickets just to listen to Judy Collins."

"Why this concert?"

"Well, ever since he and Holly broke up he gets whipper-jawed every time he hears *Send in the Clowns*."

"Oh yeah, I've seen him do it. He just stares into his beer and gets that misty, far-away look. He's such a wuss!"

They stopped talking several minutes later when they saw him returning.

Christine asked, "Why did you get here so early?"

"Well, this concert is completely sold out, and I really wanted to hear and see Judy sing. So, I bought lawn tickets, and I got here early to save these seats near the stage."

"Church pews? On the lawn?" Christine asked.

"The pavilion seats cost well over twice as much as the lawn. But these church pews are considered lawn seats, even though you can see the show, unlike most of the park."

Cherry and Jerry, a married couple whose rhyming names reminded everyone of cartoon characters, arrived just then and joined the conversation. "What happened to your face?" Cherry asked Butch.

"I've been waiting here since one o'clock. I got sunburned. I didn't think it was going to be so damned hot and sunny today! I had to pee, but I didn't dare leave the blankets because there were lots of people trying to get these seats. I put the blankets over the back of these seats to tell people that these seats are taken, and I think I saved enough for all of us. But now I really have to get something to drink. I think I'm dehydrated."

"Make sure you get some cheese and crackers to go with your whine."

"Fuck you, Jim!" Butch retorted as he flipped him the bird.

Just then Jan arrived. "Oh, I see you saved seats! These are terrific! We're just about forty-five degrees off stage left. Or is it stage right? I can never get those straight in my mind. Butch, you look awful. What the hell happened?"

Jim snorted, "Don't ask! He'll be only too happy to tell you, with way more detail than you'll ever want to hear."

"Hey, Jim! Once again with love!" Butch responded, flipping him the bird yet again, as he

THE BEST LAID PLANS...

headed off for the concession stand.

A few minutes after Butch returned with his giant Coke and a glass of white wine, Don finally showed up. "This place is amazing! I've never been here before. I saw people with blankets sitting on the lawn with a candelabra and crystal wine glasses! What's up with the pews, though?"

Cherry responded, "Well, years ago they closed an old church around here and Ravinia bought the pews and set them up right next to the reserved seating. Kind of as a gift to the community. Anyone is allowed to sit in them, but it's first come, first served. That's why Butch got here..."

"We know, we know. At one o'clock. And Lobster Boy couldn't leave to pee!" mocked Jim. Cherry gave him a dirty look.

Butch decided to hold court among his friends. "You know, Judy Collins came out and sang about six songs just to do acoustic checks at about two o'clock. I was the only one here. It was like a private concert, just for me."

Christine asked, "Did she sing IT?"

"Nope, but I know she'll do it later."

Most of Butch's friends gave each other knowing glances. They'd all seen his lower lip quiver just listening to that song. They realized for him it had become a theme song – an anthem of confusion and regret.

More people arrived, and Ravinia filled up to the brim. The show was due to start at seven o'clock, and around six-thirty a group of twenty college students arrived, each one pushing a wheelchair holding a severely handicapped person. They set the wheelchairs right next to the church pews on a slight hillside that dipped down towards the stage. They locked the hand brakes on all the wheelchairs and began to talk amongst themselves.

"Geez, what's wrong with them?" Jan asked.

Cherry hissed, "Don't stare at them, asshole!"

"I think they have cerebral palsy," Butch said. "If you look at them, just glance, don't stare, you'll notice they don't have the coordination to move their own wheelchairs. Their hands are… oh, what the hell is the word… athetoid, that's it. See how their wrists are severely bent and their fingers are kind of pushed together almost to a point?"

Jan replied, "My God, they look awful. How'd they get that way?"

"It's got something to do with lack of oxygen when they were born," Butch explained. "Weirdly, though, while their bodies are totally screwed up, they are as smart as anybody. Their muscles are so uncoordinated and stiff, it's extremely difficult for them to communicate. Most of the time their speech is barely intelligible. They even have to be fed and changed."

"My God, that's horrible. Imagine having a normal brain, but trapped in a useless body that has betrayed you."

"Yeah, we're really lucky compared to those poor bastards."

Everybody sat quietly for a few minutes. Each lost in their own depressive thoughts. Jim perked up first. He sang, mimicking a Christmas carol, "Do you smell what I smell…?" Christine punched his arm.

"I do believe, yon college students are getting stoned!" Don pointed out.

Jan sighed, "Ahhh, memories! Sweet dorm days daze!"

"Jesus, look at that!" cried Jerry, as he pointed to a college student rolling up her program and placing it to her lips. She blew marijuana smoke through the handmade tube directly into the nose and mouth of one of the handicapped women. Soon, other college students followed suit.

CAPTAIN BILLY C.

"They're shotgunning the wheelchair jockeys!" Evidently, they believed, as did Bob Dylan, that *everybody must get stoned*.

"No, I can't fuckin' believe it!" exclaimed Don. "And don't call them that – they're people too!"

"Somebody should call security! That's just not right, getting those poor handicapped people stoned," Jan said.

Jim scoffed, "Why? It's not like they're driving home. Furthermore, what difference does it make? After all, it's not going to ruin their ambition to become an astronaut. Let the poor bastards get high."

This comment caused a complete halt to all of the side conversations around them. They each appeared to ponder what Jim had said. It didn't seem right, but then again, maybe he was right. Each of them wrestled with their thoughts as the lights in the pavilion dimmed, and the stage lights grew bright. Judy Collins was suddenly illuminated by a spotlight on the stage. Everyone yelled and shouted.

With the crowd finally settled down and listening as Judy Collins sang *Both Sides Now*, the pew sitters continued to drink more and more wine. The college students continued to smoke more and more dope, and continued to shotgun the handicapped people, getting them more and more stoned.

As Judy sang through her repertoire, some of the college students started making out with each other. Butch was too much of a Judy Collins fan to participate in such an activity while she was singing. Besides, he was alone, at least when it came to female companionship. So, the opportunity could never present itself. This added to his maudlin mood.

Butch glanced over at his wheelchair-bound compatriots and was shocked. They, too, struggled to get involved, romantically. Their heads were moved closer together, but it was hard for them to kiss. One of the males struggled to get his claw-like hand on the boobs of the female in the wheelchair next to him. Butch almost spit out his semi-high-quality Rhine wine. Several of the other handicapped people began doing the same thing. The college kids just laughed.

Very few things could distract Butch and his friends from watching Judy Collins perform, but this was definitely one of them. Instead of looking slightly to the left and down on the stage, their heads were all cocked to the right, watching the stoned wheelchair-riders clumsily try to grope each other. Every mouth was agape.

As the concert neared the end, Christine piped up, "I need to pee. And I think I'm getting a contact high just from sitting here. I've got the munchies, so I'm getting an ice cream cone. Anybody else want one?"

Having no takers, she trotted off for the restrooms and the food vendors.

When she returned and sat down again, the concert ended. However, after Judy thanked the crowd and walked off-stage, the stage lights remained on and the house lights stayed dim. Whether they smoked or not, people took out their cigarette lighters and held them in the air.

Christine looked at Butch and said, "She didn't sing it!!"

Butch responded, "Patience, Obi-Won! She's coming back!"

The crowd continued to scream "MORE!"

Send in the Clowns starts with a few unique notes played on an oboe. Those notes immediately quieted the crowd. Judy's most important song was here. Butch's lower lip began to quiver in anticipation. A tear welled up in his eye. Lost loves and lost opportunities flooded his heart.

THE BEST LAID PLANS...

Unfortunately for Butch, the stoned crippled people knew this song more than the rest of Judy's repertoire and began to sing at the top of their lungs, totally off key and out of rhythm with Judy. In fact, most of them just howled various mispronunciations of the word "Clown," loud enough for Judy to glance over to see what was happening.

The crack security team rushed down the hill and screeched to an abrupt halt. One huge black man, who looked like a linebacker for the Bears, froze in mid-stride. He looked perplexed. The entire security team looked at each other and never said a word. But it was very easy to read their minds. *What the hell do I do now? I can't throw out crippled people in wheelchairs. My God, I'm not trained for this.*

Butch's friends all looked at him. The tears caused by melancholia were now replaced with tears of rage. He fumed, "I'm going to release the brakes on their wheelchairs and have them go careening down the hill into the trees!" He started to get up when Jim grabbed his arm and said, "You can't do that!" But he was laughing so hard, tears began to roll down his cheeks as well.

Christine turned to Butch and howled

"CLOWN!" and smashed the ice cream cone she was holding into her own forehead. Butch's friends literally fell out of their pews in gales of laughter.

Butch knew he had lost something at that moment. He would never have a mystical, melancholy experience listening to Judy sing his personal anthem. He thought, *Send in the clowns – don't bother, they're here.* And he never wanted to hear that fucking song again.

28. Wired for Success

AT PRECISELY 1 pm, Amanda Peterson strode purposefully into the small conference room. Three men and one woman looked up apprehensively as she entered.

"Thank you, folks, for coming. Let's get down to business. As you know, the professional electronics show is scheduled to begin in two weeks at McCormick Place. We have invested a fair amount of money to set up a booth in the display center near the entrance. I do not have to tell you, but apparently I'm going to anyway, everybody at that convention will be competing for the eyes and ears of potential investors, collaborators, and customers.

"On the bright side, we have some good and innovative products. On the dark side, few people have ever heard of Acme Electronics of Buffalo Grove, IL. So, our job is to find a way to seduce passersby to stop, look at our displays, and talk to us. To add to the complexity of the situation, our budget is somewhat limited and, consequently, we cannot produce the same glitzy, glamorous display that a company like Motorola can. Let's take a minute to think and in a few moments' time, we're going to share our ideas. We have to come up with a plan. Our company's future, and consequently our jobs, depend on it."

Amanda was a forty-something-year-old Loyola University MBA graduate who always "dressed for success." Today she wore a dove-gray jacket and skirt with a navy-blue blouse. She had a small, tasteful silver chain around her neck. Her blue pumps that matched her blouse had a small heel. While she believed in fashion, she did not believe that shoes should make you uncomfortable. She was a no-nonsense woman who did not suffer fools.

After waiting for a few moments, which allowed the tension to build, she said, "Let's go around the room and share our immediate ideas. Joe, we'll start with you. Remember, no feedback until everyone has shared their ideas. Joe…"

"We can have really big signs that show off who we are and what our products are."

"Mary…"

"How about bright, flashing lights. Something

like a visi-bar from a squad car. Or maybe even a strobe light."

"Larry..."

"We could set up video cameras so that people can see themselves on television screens."

"Phil..."

"We need a free act."

Mary questioned, "A what?"

"It's an old carnival term. We need something that will cause people to stop and stare, that you don't charge them for. A free act! The two biggest are fire and water. People will walk out of their way to stare at a fountain. They will also walk out of their way to see something on fire. There is a bar in Orlando, Florida. I think it's called Rosie O'Grady's or Church Street Station, I'm not sure which. Anyway, they have huge front doors that they always leave open and when you look in toward the rear what you see is a big tropical-looking waterfall with fire coming out of two pots on the side. It makes no sense, but everybody who walks by will stop and stare. And a lot of folks will walk all the way to the back of the bar just to see it. And obviously, once they're in the bar, might as well get a drink."

Amanda went next. "I was thinking of a give-away. Pads of paper with our company logo and phone number on them. Or maybe t-shirts, although that would get to be expensive. Any other ideas?" She paused. "No? Well, let's start critiquing."

Phil started. "Big signs are nice, but we don't have the room to compete with other big signs put up by other companies. Besides, it's 1983. Signs are so 50s."

Joe looked disheartened. But seeking to redeem himself, he pontificated, "I could see some flashing lights, but a lot of displays will have them. And I don't want us to look like we're advertising a discount store or a pawn shop. Furthermore, a strobe light…really…? Let's mimic a 70s disco while causing some poor schmo to have an epileptic seizure as he walks by."

Amanda looked at Phil and said, "While I like fire and water, Phil, there are some problems. If you remember, it wasn't all that long ago that the original McCormick Place burned to the ground. I'm not sure they'll let us have fire big enough to attract attention. We also have a problem with the water. Even if we are running recirculating pumps, it's hard to get a fountain big enough to draw people in. And the plumber's union will demand a huge fee. Even if we set it up ourselves, union rules say they must inspect everything to make sure it's 'safe,'" using air quotes. "There's a similar problem with the TV circuitry. The electrician's union would demand that they set it up. Once again for 'safety' reasons. And union labor there is neither fast nor cheap"

She glanced at her watch. "I have to take care of some other business matters. But I need a decision made ASAP. Why don't the four of you remain here and hash out your ideas. When I come back in two hours, I expect a unified proposal. Keep in mind our parameters: space, safety, and cost issues. We need the most bang for our buck. I know this is a short time period, but I need results. See you in two hours."

With that, she stood and abruptly left the meeting. Her mind was racing. *I don't know if this team is sharp enough to come up with a better way of marketing Acme Electronics at this convention. Big signs, flashing lights, a giant water fountain with fire shooting out of it...really? I haven't even had time for my lunch yet. If my blood sugar drops much more, I'm going to kill someone.*

She headed down the corridor towards her

CAPTAIN BILLY C.

office, hoping to grab a quick bite to eat, and was stopped almost immediately by Henry Johnson. *Oh, for Christ's sake, what now,* she thought. Henry was a large, black man whose bearing testified to his previous military experience. His gray, well-pressed, uniform fit him perfectly. He was everything you would want in a security officer, but without the gun. As she studied him, she realized that she barely knew the man beyond the name on his badge. Security matters didn't normally fall under her purview.

"Ms. Peterson, I hate to bother you, but Mr. Taylor is gone for the rest of the day and I need some guidance as to what to do with a situation that has come up. A boy has entered our locked, fenced-in area in the back. You know, where we keep our surplus wires and circuits that are going to be recycled."

"What was he doing there?"

"Ma'am, he was stealing a bunch of wires."

"Wires?"

"Yes, ma'am. Various sizes and lengths."

"Was he after the copper, hoping to sell it?"

"I don't think so, ma'am. There was some heavy cable there with a lot of copper and he ignored that. He was going for more of the 14 and

16 gauge. You know, the thinner stuff. We have him in the security area and I was wondering if you could go down and talk to him. He doesn't seem willing to talk to me or any of the other guards."

Amanda glanced at her watch again. "Well, I suppose I can give you a few minutes. Are you afraid he's planning on making a bomb or something?"

"Ma'am, I just don't know. The whole thing is weird. We don't even know how he got in. The gate is still locked."

While Amanda and Henry took the elevator down to the first floor, her stomach growled loudly in protest at her missed lunch. Amanda was embarrassed, but Henry either did not hear or, kindly, pretended not to notice. They proceeded to the security area, which was located adjacent to the front lobby. Upon entering the room, she saw a shaggy-haired, skinny, blonde teenager slouched on an office chair. He looked up at her with a bored expression on his face. He had on worn, black jeans and a black, Motley Crue t-shirt. The smell of stale cigarette smoke, with just a hint of marijuana, emanated from his clothing.

Amanda decided to take a motherly approach to him. "Son, can you explain what you were doing on our property?"

"I ain't your son and you ain't my mother."

She paused. *Well, that didn't work. I'll have to try something else.* She started over. "OK. Young man, please explain what you were doing on our property."

"Lookin' for stuff."

"This is private property. You know, I could call the police and have you arrested for breaking and entering."

"I didn't break into anything."

"The gate is locked. How did you get on to our property?"

"Nice job on locking things up. Let me give you a tip. If you're going to lock the gate with a chain and padlock, don't leave it so loose. If you push on the gate just a little, you can just slip through."

"Good to know." She gave Henry a reprimanding look. "I could have you arrested for trespassing."

"Oh no! Not the police! They'll probably give me thirty years hard labor at Joliet. Or maybe even the electric chair," he scoffed. "Who are you kidding lady? I'm sixteen."

Amanda was flustered. She was used to people being intimidated by her intelligence and her take-charge attitude. Having no children of her own, she was certainly not used to the insolent attitude he was displaying. She tried again. "Can you at least tell me your name?"

"Donny."

Oh, my God. It's like pulling teeth! "Donny, may I have your last name?" she queried, clenching her jaw.

"McNamara."

"Thank you. Now, Donny, I understand you took some of our lighter gauge wires. What did you intend to do with them?"

"Make stuff."

She glanced over at Henry with a look that said, *hold me back so I don't kill this little son-of-a-bitch*. Henry nodded to her while trying to stifle a smirk. To Amanda, it was clear that he was enjoying seeing her totally out of her element. And she had to admit that Loyola, while an excellent university, never prepared her for dealing with a surly teenager.

Once again, she continued. "Donny, would you mind being more specific as to WHAT you were trying to make." She was still worried about the possibility of a bomb.

"I guess."

"Well..."

"I was going to make animals."

Her and Henry's jaws dropped. Of all the possible answers they could have anticipated, animals never made the list.

"Animals? What kind of animals do you make?"

"Wire animals."

Only social norms and a life-long practice of controlling her emotions kept her fingers from flying around Donny's throat and choking the living shit out of him. "Donny, I'm sorry, I'm lost. I don't understand what you are talking about. Can you show me?"

Donny sighed heavily. "OK. Tell Dudley Do-Right over there to give me back my wire," gesturing toward Henry.

Amanda was going to say, "*It's not your wire, it's our wire. And don't be so disrespectful to Mr. Johnson, you little shit.*" But she stopped herself, took a deep breath, and resignedly said, "fine," and motioned for Donny to go over to the desk where the wires were jumbled together.

Henry and Amanda watched as Donny sorted through the wire and made several piles based on length and size. After assessing his options, Donny picked up a fairly thin, solid strand of pink wire and started bending it rapidly. In less than a minute he had created a two-inch tall frog. He put it on Henry's desk and said, "If you push down on his back by his butt, he jumps."

Donny reached out and pressed his thumb down on the frog. The frog sprang into the air and flew almost all the way across the desk. Henry snatched it up just as it was about to tumble off the edge. "Well, I'll be Goddamned," he exclaimed and then caught himself. "Oh, sorry, Ms. Peterson."

Amanda stood there in shock for a moment and then asked, "Can you make anything else?"

A smile lit up Donny's face as his attitude changed. He rapidly grabbed another piece of wire and made a moose.

Amanda picked up the frog and said in amazement, "There are no false bends in this sculpture! How do you do this?"

"I don't know. I just make things."

"How many different animals can you make?"

"I don't know. I never counted them. A bunch.

I can also make a swing set."

"A what?"

"You know, a playground swing set. But I need a pair of wire cutters or maybe nail clippers."

Henry said, "I think I have a pair in my desk." He gave the clippers to Donny.

This piece was far more elaborate. But in the end, there was a playground swing set with two swings that could easily rock back and forth, just like the real thing. Donny was now warming up to his audience. "It takes a while, but I can make an eagle and a duck."

Amanda had a faraway look in her eye. When she refocused, she said, "Donny, how old are you?"

"I already told you. Sixteen."

"Hmmm. Do you want a job?"

"A job? Doing what?"

"Making animals, Donny. Just making animals."

"Yeah, sure. I guess so."

Two Weeks Later

ACME ELECTRONICS' CONVENTION display was a

huge hit. The conventioneers loved watching Donny, spotlighted on an elevated platform, make animals. He was, after all, a "free act." And while the conventioneers watched Donny, Acme's representatives could talk to them about investment and collaborative opportunities. Once the animals were completed, they were given to those people who showed the most interest in the electronics company, along with the "mandatory" tri-fold brochure.

Phil looked at Amanda and said, "Wow, this worked out perfectly. And the nice part is that even though we're using wires, we don't have to give a damned dime to the electrician's union. We're really wired for success!"

About the Author

CAPTAIN BILLY HAS always loved the water. It didn't matter to him whether it was organizing a rafting trip on rapids, racing his homebuilt hydroplane, leisurely sailing, or taking one of his several powerboats on lakes or intercoastal waterways. Over the years he has taken hundreds of people with him, often regaling them with stories of shipwrecks, island hermits, pirates, buried treasure, and the ecology of the area. Some of his stories were even true! It is in this way that he became affectionately known as "the Captain."

Even when out of the water, Captain Billy has always been a storyteller. If he were Irish, it would have been said he "kissed the Blarney Stone" and was "blessed with the gift of gab." If he were rich and sophisticated, people would have said that he was "glib." But since he is Italian, people just say he is full of "bull."

Throughout his entire life, he has chosen to tell stories in many different ways. He took Improv classes at Second City and Victory

Gardens theaters in Chicago. He acted in a play and discovered that, although he liked being on stage, he was, to quote Shakespeare, "a poor player." For some odd reason, he could never remember his lines. At one time he had his own basic cable TV show and discovered he could work many hours and make absolutely no money. Later, he moved up to being an extra in a "for real" Hollywood movie and made a whopping $75 (before taxes) in a mere ten hours. His only scene has him looking out a bus window with seventeen other guys being sent to prison. It lasts almost three seconds. He realized he could make more money at Walmart as a greeter. He did a stand-up comedy routine at a local comedy club, just to see if he had the guts to do it. And although the routine went very well, he learned that he would have to work way too hard to take it to the next level. And being the couch potato that he is, that thought ended his meteoric comedy career.

Captain Billy planned to perform and tell stories the rest of his life, but the best laid plans... Unfortunately for the Captain, in 2001 he was diagnosed with throat cancer and had to endure months of surgery, chemotherapy, and radiation.

Fortunately, he had weekends off. The chemo and radiation caused him to lose all his hair and he described himself as looking like a thumb.

But Captain Billy survived. The good news is that he is far healthier than he should be given his age and aggressively sedentary lifestyle. The bad news is that the aftereffects of the radiation partially paralyzed his tongue and gifted him with a speech impediment. Captain Billy always sounds like he is drunk, which is sad because he does not drink. Consequently, he suffers some of the side effects of drinking without any of the fun.

He mourned the loss of his ability to tell stories. Until he realized he could write them. And write them, he did. His first book, *50 Ways to Be a Mainer*, is a collection of fifty humorous essays about what life is like in Maine. An excerpt from the book follows. But still wanting to tell more stories, he wrote *The Best Laid Plans...* This second book contains twenty-eight fun stories about people making plans that go awry. All twenty-eight stories are based on real-life experiences that Captain Billy collected from acquaintances, friends, and family members.

Humor has always been an important part of the Captain's storytelling. He fervently hopes that you will find that his two books bring a smile to your face, a chuckle to your voice, and brighten your day.

Excerpt from 50 Ways to Be a Mainer

The Joke's On You

MAINERS HAVE A great sense of humor. It's just different. While New Yorkers enjoy rapid fire jokes, Mainers like to draw out each and every joke and turn it into a personal story that lasts far longer than most other Americans would tolerate.

Henny Youngman was famous for delivering very short, unrelated jokes. For example, "A guy walks into a psychiatrist's office. He says, 'Doc, I'm thinking of killing myself.' The doctor says, 'OK, pay in advance.'" Or perhaps his most famous, and probably the shortest joke in the English language, "Take my wife, please!" Another example is Rodney Dangerfield, who turned self-deprecatory humor into an art form. "When I was twelve, my family moved to Miami. When I was seventeen, I found them." Both of these jokes and these comedians' style pay homage to Mies van der Rohe who said, "less is more." They use the least number of words possible to deliver the punch line.

Maine humor involves long, detailed storytelling. The voyage is as important as the destination. Mainers are content to sit patiently as the story meanders its way to its humorous conclusion. Allow me to give you an example of an actual joke told by one of the local residents: "Well, I wuz driving on Route 2 past the ol' red hay barn, that burnt down seven years ago, when I got to a detour caused by seasonal road construction. Well, they had so many barricades and orange cones and blinking yellow lights, it became quite the puzzler and I kinda got lost. Nothin' looked familiar, and it was gettin' late. So, I drove past a blueberry field and saw a huge white tent in front of a gray cedar-shingled farmhouse with green shutters and a gray roof. I drove up the gravel driveway, stepped out my truck, and approached a man in a freshly pressed red plaid shirt who looked to be in his sixties. I said, 'looks like you're having a pah-ty.' He said, 'Ayuh. My dad's getting remarried to a twenty-two-year-old.' I said, 'Gosh, almighty, how old's your dad?' He said, 'Well, next summah he'll be ninety-two.' I said, 'Mercy, why would a man who is gonna be ninety-two next summah want to marry a twenty-two-year-old?' The man shook his head and replied, 'He didn't want to, he had to.' "

Believe it or not, I shortened that joke. In the comedic world, this is known as a "shaggy dog" story. The more details, the better. A shaggy dog story is a long, meandering tale where the importance lies in keeping the audience's attention for as long as possible before delivering a punch line that may be irrelevant to the entire story. Many popular Maine humorists have created whole personas as they share their rambling stories, such as Marshall Dodge's *Bert and I* (famous for the phrase "you can't get theah from heah") and Clyde Folsom's *Claude Frechette*.

Although the two aforementioned gentlemen made a career of telling these stories, they are not the only ones who are willing to share their humor. I have heard absolutely hysterical stories that dragged on interminably at Rotary meetings, church, and even once at a wedding reception as part of a toast to the bride. The jokes are, in many ways, similar to Mainer's driving habits. "Slow down, take your time, we ain't in no hurry to get theah."

It would be foolish to consider Maine's slow style of joke telling to be indicative of a lack of intelligence or wit. Nothing could be further from the truth. For example, a Texan was bragging about the size of his ranch. He said, "I can get up early in the morning and drive in one direction all day and not get the end of my ranch." The Mainer looked at him and said, "Ayuh, had a pick-up truck like that once myself."

To order your copy of
50 Ways to Be a Mainer, visit:
www.facebook.com/CaptainBillyC

Made in the USA
Coppell, TX
11 August 2021